Magic for Every Occasion

Also by Graham Reed
MAGICAL MIRACLES YOU CAN DO

GRAHAM REED

MAGIC
FOR EVERY
OCCASION

ILLUSTRATED BY DENNIS PATTEN

ELSEVIER / NELSON BOOKS
New York

Gratitude is expressed to Waddingtons Playing Card
Co, Ltd, who kindly gave permission for
copyrighted playing-card designs to be used in some of
the illustrations in this book.

LIBRARY OF CONGRESS CATALOGING IN PUBLICATION DATA
Reed, Graham.   Magic for every occasion.
Includes index.
Summary: Gives step-by-step instructions for magic tricks appropriate for
specific occasions. Also includes a dictionary of magic terms and a list of
recommended tricks for sale.
1. Tricks—Juvenile literature.   2. Conjuring—
Juvenile literature.   [1. Magic tricks]   I. Patten, Dennis.   II. Title.
GV1548.R39   1981   793.8   81-3116
ISBN 0-525-66733-4   AACR2

Published in the United States by Elsevier-Dutton Publishing Co., Inc.,
2 Park Avenue, New York, N.Y. 10016.
Printed in the U.S.A. First U. S. edition
10 9 8 7 6 5 4 3 2 1

To Timothy and Debbie
with all my love

CONTENTS

About This Book

During my twenty-five years as a magical performer, numerous people have asked me to teach them a few simple tricks. Their aims have been varied: parents wanting to amuse children, teachers and youth-club leaders eager to discover new ways to stimulate young minds, teenagers with show-business ambitions, businessmen wishing to improve their social abilities. The list goes on and on.

This constant demand indicated the need for a book, and *Magic for Every Occasion* was born. From the start I was determined to provide a practical book of audience-tested tricks. On the following pages you will find a hand-picked selection of tricks from all over the world. Many are magical classics, others, recent creations; but whatever their history, they all have two points in common—they are baffling and they are entertaining.

You may be wondering how I can justify releasing so many hitherto closely guarded secrets. Is it ethical? Will members of The Magic Circle object? The answer is simple: I believe that books that are padded with useless tricks are far more damaging to magic (and to the reader) than books that show you how to do a few good tricks and how to do them well. People who read *Magic for Every Occasion* are not doing so merely to find out how tricks work. On the contrary, they want to entertain audiences and I, for my part, will do everything I can to help them succeed. Obviously I will not expose the exclusive tricks used by professional performers; I would only ruin your fun and damage their livelihood.

I also believe the average reader of this book doesn't want to be confronted with paragraph after paragraph of in-depth thinking about audience psychology and related topics. I have tried, therefore, to condense the points I believe to be important into lists of Golden Rules at the beginning of each chapter. Some of them are repeated in a Final Thoughts section at the end of every chapter. Please read them carefully—they will help you to be a polished magical entertainer.

Although the book is written for the person who performs relatively infrequently, I have tried to provide information that will enable you to increase your magical activities should you so desire. Deceivers' Dictionary is an essential list of magical jargon that will help you to read conjuring books more advanced than this one. Tested Trickery shows you how to spend your money wisely, how to buy tricks that are good value for your money. These two chapters (plus Useful Addresses and Recommended Reading) will act as a valuable source of knowledge and a signpost for the future.

Finally my loving thanks to Barbara, my wife, for spending hours and hours typing the book.

I hope you enjoy it.

GRAHAM REED
(Associate of the Inner Magic Circle)

THE
SECRET
OF MAGIC

Although this book is written, primarily, for the person who may wish to perform only occasionally, I believe you will have so much fun that you will want to become more involved in a pastime that has everything. I say this with good reason because conjuring gives you such wonderful opportunities to enjoy yourself:

You can *perform* magic and amaze your friends;

You can *invent* new tricks and baffle other magicians;

You can *design,* and make, novel illusions and create a unique act;

You can *write* articles for specialist conjuring magazines and gain the respect of entertainers all over the world;

You can *collect* old props and books and discover that history can be exciting!

You can *earn* cash in your spare time;

You can *entertain* the aged;

You can *donate* your services to deserving charities;

You can *meet* international show-business celebrities;

The list is never ending.

Conjuring is a participative pastime—you are actively involved rather than a mere spectator; and you will find that public performing gives your self-confidence a tremendous boost. You will also discover that the knowledge of psychology needed to anticipate audience reaction helps your normal day-to-day relationships with friends and business colleagues.

Furthermore, conjuring can be an inexpensive hobby—and it's suitable for any age from eight to eighty—male or female. It's truly fun for all the family.

If you become a true enthusiast you may wish to join a magical society—and there are quite a few in the world. Some demand a high standard of ability before you are accepted as a member, but most of them are usually sympathetic if you have "the magic bug." Many societies have annual shows and conventions which provide the opportunity to see first-class magicians at work. My own interest in magic was encouraged and stimulated by the members of the Middlesbrough Circle of Magicians, of which I am proud to be a past president. A move down to the south of England then gave me the opportunity to join the world famous Magic Circle in London, where I have made many friends who have helped me tremendously. A personal thank you to all of you in Middlesbrough and The Magic Circle.

Obviously a great deal of secrecy surrounds conjuring, and the newcomer often has trouble obtaining advice from people more experienced than he is. With this in mind I have asked several talented magical entertainers to outline a few hints and tips which, in their opinion, are of importance. Some points are duplicated, and I think the repetition highlights the ground rules that must be observed if success is to be achieved. Whether you perform infrequently or regularly, the following comments are invaluable.

Before introducing my guest contributors, I will start the section with a few thoughts of my own.

My first point appears several times in this book: Please *don't* perform unless you are absolutely sure the time and place are suitable. Many amateur magicians, flushed with enthusiasm for a new trick, force it on their unsuspecting friends, who are usually too polite to object. It's far better to be known as a reluctant performer, for whom it's worth waiting than being considered a bore who should be avoided.

Even if you perform infrequently, always be sure your tricks are polished to perfection. There is no excuse for sloppiness. Each trick should be rehearsed several times before it is performed in public. Try to add improvements of your own: how can the trick be made more entertaining, more mysterious, more dramatic, more colorful?

Magic is a means to an end, not the end itself. Primarily you are an entertainer using conjuring as your means. A trick is not necessarily entertaining merely because it is baffling: on the other hand, a light-hearted stunt shouldn't be ignored because it isn't mysterious.

Whether you are performing a few card tricks or a full routine onstage, your *patter* (the words you speak during your act) is of vital importance. Too many magicians merely describe the trick they are performing: "Here is a pack of cards. Take a card, and place it back in the pack," et cetera. How much better to say: "Ladies and gentlemen, let me now show you a miracle with a pack of cards; it was taught to me by a gambler from Las Vegas; it earned him a lot of money."

My first contributor is Peter Leonard, who has been performing magic for thirty years (he insists he started very young!). He lives in Cleveland and frequently entertains at parties for children. For adults he presents a light-hearted mind-reading act.

Magic is an entertaining mystery, or a mysterious entertainment.

If you mystify without entertaining, no one will want to watch your magic.

If you entertain without mystifying, you cannot call yourself a magician.

The means by which your magic is achieved should be as unnoticeable as possible.

Misdirection should divert attention away from the means.

Treat your audience with courtesy. If you need audience participation, remember the assistants are your guests. They are doing you a favor. Do not embarrass them or make them uncomfortable in any way. This rule applies to children just as much as to adults.

Your personality will determine the way you present magic; do not copy another person's presentations. Apart from making you unpopular, their presentation cannot fit your own personality—it will be obviously false. Develop your own style.

My second contributor is Rex Cooper, who is a member of the Inner Magic Circle (with gold star) and a member of the International Brotherhood of Magicians. He is a well-known children's entertainer, and he is also a skilled close-up performer.

When you have chosen the effect or routine which you wish to perform, rehearse it until you know the whole thing thoroughly. Think of everything that could go wrong and devise ways to get out of the situation. What will you say if you drop a prop—or if somebody starts to heckle you? Be prepared for every eventuality.

Show your routine to a sympathetic friend before giving a public performance. Take note of the reaction you receive and adjust your actions or patter, accordingly. Try to learn something from each performance. Try to find ways to improve your tricks constantly. Practice your facial expressions, make sure they are natural and occur at the appropriate time.

It takes a long time to create a good magical routine. Don't be tempted to do a trick until you are sure it is ready for your public.

My third contributor is Alan Taylor, who is a teacher by day and a magical entertainer in his spare time. He has performed in numerous clubs the length and breadth of England. His act of comedy magic has been seen on television. He has created several tricks and, for a while, helped to run a magical-supply business in the north of England.

To develop an *entertaining* magical act involves a lot of hard work, but I can assure you it brings its own rewards.

There isn't an easy road to success. You must practice hard—and then gain experience.

Practice is essential. It enables your performance to become second nature, leaving you free to concentrate on entertaining your audience—to develop your style, your own personality. Your act (whether one trick or ten) must flow smoothly. Every prop should have a place, and every prop should be *in* its place.

As far as possible, make certain a trick cannot go wrong. Even if you perform only once a year, make that performance as professional as you can.

Gain as much experience as you can, perform for charities and other organizations that will welcome an entertainer. Each time you perform a trick make it a good amateur learning experience. Analyze your show: how could it have been improved?

My next contributor is Dennis Patten, who, apart from having contributed the illustrations in this book, is also a professional magician. He specializes in entertaining children, and his mysterious tricks, colorful props, and easygoing manner all combine to provide a show that kids love. Dennis tells us what conjuring means to him:

I have been a magical enthusiast for over thirty years, and in that time conjuring has meant many different things to me.

As an eleven-year-old it was an absorbing fun hobby. I spent hours learning new tricks and searching book shops and libraries for books on conjuring. Magic books, in those days, mainly consisted of descriptions of magical props, and the enthusiast had to make up routines as best he could. It's so much easier these days, with books providing so much valuable information.

As a teenager magic brought me the friendship of others interested in the art. Later, in my job as a technical representative, the ability to do a few tricks helped me to break the ice at many business interviews. As a parent it has helped to amuse and entertain my small daughters and their friends.

I have been a professional magician for twenty years. I have the magic bug—I eat, drink and sleep magic!

My words of advice are few: Don't hesitate—become interested in magic *now*. But practice hard—even the simplest trick deserves to be performed well. I can promise you a lot of fun. Best of luck.

My last contributor is Paul Daniels, the best-known and brightest magical entertainer in Britain. Paul and I have been friends for twenty years, and in that time he has become a celebrity. Paul has had tremendous experience in showbusiness. His catch phrase "You'll like this—not a lot—but you'll like it" can be heard everywhere you go, a testimony to Paul's popularity. Paul Daniels is, without doubt, a star, and magic is proud of him.

If magic is to be magical, then it needs to be entertaining. If the audience, whether one or one thousand, is not entertained, their minds will wander and you will fail to capture their hearts.

The secret of making magic entertaining has always seemed to me to be very simple, and yet most performers seem to find what I am about to advise very difficult indeed.

The secret is this: It is essential that you, as a performer, *be yourself*. That is to say that when you are on stage, or doing a trick at home for a few friends, *do not* assume a voice that you do not use normally; do not take on airs and graces you do not normally possess; do not adopt mannerisms you don't use in everyday life. Relax and enjoy what you are doing, and the audiences will relax and enjoy it with you. They will sense any falseness or strain, no matter how hard you try to conceal it. If you are a naturally funny person, you should perform in a funny way; if you are normally serious, then be a serious performer. It is wrong to say that the tricks do not matter, but you and your approach matter so much more. So the secret of success, I believe, is: relax, be yourself, and enjoy your performing.

Have fun.

GAGS FOR
A SOCIAL
GATHERING

The friendly atmosphere of a social gathering often prompts your pals to say "Show us a trick." This chapter contains a fair selection of stunts, puzzles, gags, and minor miracles.

GOLDEN RULE

Generally speaking, people at a social gathering make a happy, cheerful, and enthusiastic audience. **Don't let this encouraging atmosphere persuade you to overstay your welcome.**

◀ Instant Coin Vanish

There are many ways to vanish a coin, and most of them are very difficult. The Instant Coin Vanish is, however, relatively simple and extremely baffling.

You need two identical small coins—dimes or pennies. They must be exactly alike—same date, same condition. Prepare the trick by placing one of the coins in your otherwise empty right trouser pocket; the audience must not be aware of this advance preparation.

To perform the trick, show the other coin and place it against your trousers, holding it (in your right hand) as shown in figure 1. The back of the right hand is resting against the part of your trousers immediately next to the coin in your pocket. With your left hand fold a portion of material over the visible coin (figure 2.) As you do this, and when the coin is covered by the fold of cloth, curl your right fingers into your right palm, taking the coin with them. At the same time turn the back of your hand to the audience and point with your right forefinger toward the fold of cloth (see figure 3). Your left hand presses down on the fold of cloth and grips the coin in your pocket. The illusion is perfect, it looks as though you were holding the previously visible coin, which is now (unknown to the audience) being firmly held against your right palm by your right fingertips. With your left fingers start to rub the cloth above the coin, slowly releasing your grip. Eventually the cloth will straighten out—the coin has vanished.

Ask somebody to reach into your pocket and remove the coin. It seems that it has "visibly" penetrated the cloth of your trousers!

The startling climax gives you plenty of opportunity to drop the coin in your right hand secretly into your jacket pocket.

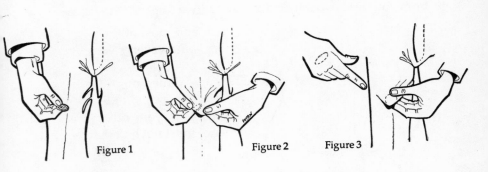

Figure 1   Figure 2   Figure 3

☛ Frustrating Crossword Puzzle

You will drive your friends crazy with this silly little puzzle:

CLUES: *Across*   *Down*   Figure 4

B	I	T	E
B	I	T	E
B	I	T	E
B	I	T	E

(1) Dogs do it.   (1) Buzzing insects.
(2) Fleas do it.   (2) Organs of vision.
(3) Snakes do it.   (3) To annoy; to provoke.
(4) Lions do it.   (4) Comfort.

The answer: Just write the word BITE on the four horizontal lines—the Down words will then be apparent.

☛ The Jumping Rubber Band

A mysterious "quickie."

Place a rubber band around the first and second fingers of your left hand (see figure 5). Turn your hand back upward and clench it into a fist. As you do so, place all four fingertips inside the rubber band (figure 6) *without* letting the audience see you do so. Use your right hand to help place the band in position. Keeping the back of your hand toward the audience, straighten your fingers and the rubber band will visibly jump from your first two fingers to your last two fingers! (See figure 7.)

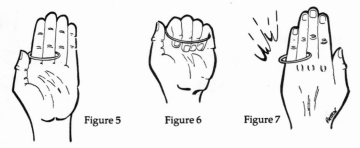

Figure 5   Figure 6   Figure 7

☛ Pocket Calculator

Another amusing gag. Out of cardboard or plywood make a "pocket calculator" (figure 8).

Tell your friends it is a new kind of pocket calculator. How do you use it? Simply stick your fingers through the holes and count 1—2—3—4—5.

Figure 8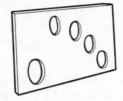

Figure 9

☛ Which Object?

Ask somebody to hold a dime in his right hand and a penny in his left.

Turn your back and ask your helper to think of one of the two coins. As an aid to concentration, ask him to hold the hand containing that coin against his forehead.

Tell your assistant the trick relies on his deep, intense concentration—without his help the trick will fail. Turn around again (before doing so, ask the assistant to lower his hand)—you can now correctly divine the coin on which he was concentrating.

How do you do it?

The answer is simple: Glance at his hands and one will be *slightly* lighter in color than the other. The paler hand is the one the spectator held against his forehead. Name the coin in that hand and enjoy another triumph!

Incidentally, the hand is paler in color because it is partly drained of blood. Consequently, the longer the assistant holds his hand against his forehead the more noticeable will be the color contrast between his two hands.

📣 Antigravity Matches

A simple trick, but worth including in a close-up routine. The effect is straightforward and visual. You show a partly open box of matches; turn it upside down, and remove the drawer. Even though the matches can be heard rattling in the drawer, they don't fall out! The performer mutters a magic word and all the matches cascade onto the table. The trick depends on a secret gimmick (a broken match) that is wedged across the drawer of the matchbox (see figure 10). When you perform the trick the drawer can be partly opened without revealing the gimmick.

When the drawer is held upside down, the matches can be rattled without their falling out. A squeeze on the ends of the box will dislodge the gimmick and the matches will drop to the table.

Ideally the matchbox should then be used for another trick. A good follow-up is the Quick Coin Vanish.

Figure 10

*   *   *

☞ Quick Coin Vanish

This is a nice way to vanish a small coin, a penny, for example. You need a small empty matchbox and, of course, the coin. To perform the trick open the matchbox, drop the coin inside, and close the box. Shake the box several times and, as you do so, secretly turn it upside down.

If you hold the box by one end between the base of your thumb and forefinger and squeeze gently (see figure 11), the box will gape sufficiently to allow the coin to slide into the palm of your hand, where it can be concealed from view. Place the box in an ashtray and burn it. The coin has vanished!

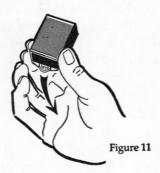

Figure 11

☞ Button Off

You could die with your boots on if you pick the wrong person for this amusing gag:

You need four men's suit buttons, one gray, one black, one brown, and one navy blue. Put the buttons in your right jacket pocket.

When you have found somebody who wears a suit with buttons in one of those colors, secretly remove a matching button from your pocket and keep it, concealed from view, in the curled fingers of your right hand.

Stand directly in front of your victim and hold the button side of his jacket (the left side as you look at him) with your right hand, the thumb on top and the fingers underneath. The button is under the cloth, still on your fingers, and it's held in place by the pressure of your thumb.

Point to a suit button with your left hand and move your right hand close to this button(keeping the loose button out of sight under the material of the jacket). *Quickly* fold part of the spectator's jacket over the suit button and pull upward, as dramatically as you can, with your right hand, displaying the loose button—it looks as if you had pulled the button off the suit!

Make a throwing motion toward the spectator's jacket, concealing the loose button in your right hand and releasing your left-hand grip on his jacket: the button has returned.

Although the trick isn't difficult to perform, it *does* need courage and a certain amount of showmanship.

☛ Tumbler Puzzler (1)

Place six glasses on a table (or bar); the first three contain liquid, the others are empty. Challenge your friends to move only *one* glass and end up with the glasses alternately full and empty. How do you do it? Empty glass 2 into glass 5 and place glass 2 back into position—and then run!

☛ Tumbler Puzzler (2)

Place three glasses on the table (see figure 12). Tell a friend you will make three moves—moving two glasses at a time—and end up with all the glasses mouth down.

Figure 12

Quickly reverse glasses 2 and 3; then 1 and 3; and finally 2 and 3 again—all the glasses should be mouth down.

Reset the glasses on the table *but* this time as shown in figure 13. Now challenge your friend to duplicate your movements, ending up with the glasses mouth down—it's impossible.

Figure 13

☛ Watch . . . Watch . . . Watch

Drape a large handkerchief or napkin over your left wrist and say "Watch . . . watch . . . watch . . ." in a very mysterious way. Then quickly pull the cloth away, revealing—a watch!

Figure 14

☛ It's Worth a Fortune

I used to have the following puzzle printed on my business cards and I was once asked for as many of my cards as I could spare because "they're worth a fortune in pints of beer"! Using a paper punch, put a small hole in the top corner of one of your cards (see figure 15).

Challenge somebody to "push a 50-cent coin through the hole without bending or tearing the card." Hopefully they will be unable to do so. You can do it by pushing the coin *through* the hole, using a pencil (figure 16).

Figure 15

Figure 16

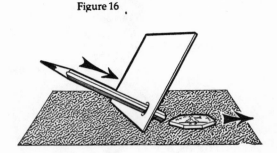

☛ Ever-Ready Coin Vanish

I like this coin vanish—it's easy to perform and very mystifying. Hold a coin in your left fingertips and, with your right hand, drape a large handkerchief over your left hand and coin. However, as you do so, secretly clip the coin between the tips of your right forefinger and middle finger (figure 17). Hold your left fingers as though the coin were still in your left hand and pull the handkerchief toward your body, all the time looking intently at your handkerchief-covered left hand.

Quickly shout "It's gone!" and pull the handkerchief away from your left hand, at the same time dropping the coin into your top pocket (figure 18). The coin has dramatically disappeared.

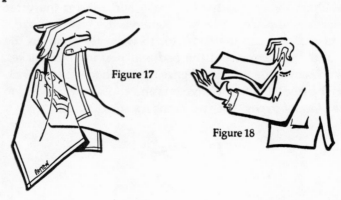

Figure 17

Figure 18

☛ Number Prediction

Present this trick with showmanship. It is suitable for a small group or even the largest theater.

You need a small, pocket note pad with identical front and back covers. On the *back* page write three 3-digit numbers. Make it look as if they had been written by three different people (see figure 19). Assuming the numbers are written in (say) black ball-point, make certain you have the same pen with you when you perform the trick. Add up the three numbers and write their total on a piece of paper that should be sealed inside an envelope. Put the envelope in your pocket.

To perform the trick tell your audience you need three volunteers who are in tune with your body. Take the pulse of several spectators—reject one or two (pulse too slow/fast), finally ending up with three suitable people.

Open the note pad to the *first* page and ask each of your three helpers to write a 3-digit number—give them your pen.

Take the pad and pen back and say your want a human computer. Take the pulse of two more spectators and select somebody a reasonable distance from your other three assistants. Open the pad to the *back* page and ask for the three numbers to be added together. Remove the envelope from your pocket and ask the spectator to write the total on the front of the envelope. Put the pad and pen in your pocket. Show the envelope to the audience, pointing to the total written on the front. Open the envelope and show your prediction on the piece of paper. The two numbers are identical!

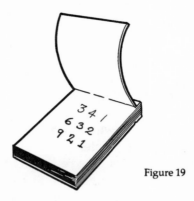

Figure 19

☞ Solid through Solid

My father used to baffle me with this effective trick, in which two matches seem visibly to pass through each other. Hold a match between the thumb and forefinger of each hand—and link the two matches (see figure 20). Tell the audience you will now move your hands apart and the matches will dissolve through each other!

To perform the trick, secretly wet the tip of your forefinger. You will find the *head* end of a match will stick to the finger, enabling you to remove your thumb for a fraction of a second without letting the match fall to the floor (figure 21). The small gap between your thumb and the end of the match is big enough for the other match to pass through. Perform the trick quickly, and it's truly baffling.

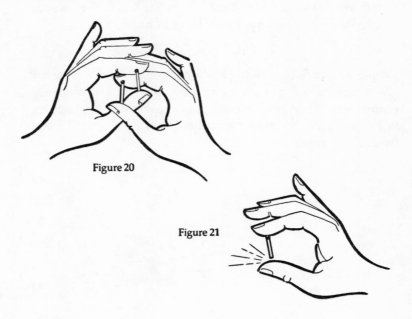

Figure 20

Figure 21

☛ Ash of the Devil

This weird trick can be given quite a spooky presentation if the atmosphere is suitable.

To prepare the trick, secretly dampen the end of your right middle finger and press it, firmly, into an ashtray. The end of the finger will be covered with cigarette ash. Ask a woman spectator to help you and shake her by the hand—as you do so, press the end of your middle finger into her palm. Unknown to the audience or your volunteer, this action will leave a deposit of ash on her hand.

Ask her to hold her right hand palm down and clench it into a fist.

Borrow a lighted cigarette and knock some ash onto the palm of your hand. Blow the ash, on your hand, in the direction of your assistant. Ask her to open her hand. The ash has mysteriously traveled from your hand to hers!

FINAL THOUGHTS

People at a social gathering are a relaxed audience; they are always interested in your magic, are cheerful and sincerely enthusiastic about your talents. This encouraging atmosphere is like a dream to most performers, but be warned: *Don't* overstay your welcome.

EASY MAGIC
FOR A
DINNER PARTY

The mellow moments following an enjoyable meal often provide the ideal atmosphere for a few impromptu tricks. This chapter contains a good selection of tried-and-tested magic.

GOLDEN RULES

Try to anticipate the occasions when you will be asked to show a few tricks—and be prepared. Planning, in advance, the tricks you intend to perform will help you to give a polished show.

Select appropriate tricks for the atmosphere in which you will be entertaining. For example, a serious, sophisticated trick would be completely unsuitable at a boisterous party. On the other hand, a light-hearted stunt may not be welcome in a more somber gathering!

A further word of caution: Keep your routine short. Remember the Golden Rule of Show Business—leave them wanting more.

☛ The Double-Value Match

This is more of a quick stunt rather than a world-shattering mystery. It is, however, an effective novelty, and it shouldn't be ignored. Your preparation is simple: Take two wooden matches and dip their heads, and part of the wooden portion of the matches, in black ink. Let the ink dry and put the matches in your pocket.

When you are seated at a dinner table, secretly drop the matches into the ashtray. They will soon become covered with ash and look just like used matches.

At an appropriate moment tell your fellow diners that many matches will strike twice if they are handled with care. Pick up one of your prepared matches and strike it. A miracle—it lights! Pick up the second match and ask someone else to hold it. This person, too, will succeed when he or she strikes it. If anybody else tries it with any other matches, he will have problems.

☛ The Vanishing Coin

Here is a neat coin vanish. You need a glass tumbler, a cloth napkin, and a borrowed small coin. I will assume you are seated at a table.

Hold the tumbler on the palm of your left hand. The coin is held in your right fingertips, and your right hand is covered with the napkin

Move the right hand until the draped napkin covers the tumbler in your left hand. Tell the audience you will drop the coin into the tumbler. As you say this, tilt the tumbler to one side (see figure 1). Drop the coin, which will hit the *outside* of the tumbler and fall into your left hand so that the coin rattles against the bottom of the tumbler on top of the coin, while, with your right hand, you quickly pull the napkin away from the tumbler. Drop the napkin onto the table and, with your right hand again, throw the tumbler into the air, shouting, as

Figure 1

you do so: "The coin has vanished." All this excitement gives you plenty of opportunity to drop the coin secretly from your left hand onto your lap, where it can later be retrieved and put in your pocket.

☛ Match Magic

Now for another of my favorite "quickies."

All you need is a book of paper matches containing about eight or nine matches.

Before you show the trick, open the matches and bend one match downward (see figure 2). As you hold the book of matches, your left thumb conceals this extra match. Show the open book of matches to somebody (keeping the extra match hidden) and ask him to count the matches. We will assume your helper says "eight."

Tear out one of the matches and place it on the table, saying, as you do so, "And that leaves seven."

Close the book of matches by folding it toward your left palm (using your right hand). This places the extra match into the book, which should now have the flap tucked in—your dinner partners will not have the opportunity to see that an extra match has been added.

Place the closed matchbook on the table.

Pick up the single match and tell your audience it is a phoenix match—able to survive flames. Strike the match and let it burn down completely. Make a mysterious pass toward the book of matches saying, "There *were* seven matches, let us see if the phoenix match has returned."

Ask somebody to count the matches—there are eight—the phoenix match has survived again!

Figure 2

☞ The-Torn-and-Restored-Napkin

This is a magical classic that has survived the test of time.

You are seated at a table and paper napkins are available.

To prepare the trick, secretly crumple a napkin and place it on your lap.

To perform the trick, take a napkin and ask someone to tear it in half. Then ask your helper to put the two halves together and tear the napkin into quarters—and to keep on tearing the napkin as small as possible. All this activity gives you plenty of opportunity to pick the napkin secretly off your lap and hold it in the curled fingers of your right hand (see figure 3).

When your assistant has finished tearing the napkin, ask him or her to roll the pieces into a ball. Take the balled napkin in your left hand and then transfer it to your right hand. Press it against the one already there. The two balled napkins can be openly displayed—they look like one.

Ask another spectator to pass you the pepper shaker—but before he does so, would he please make sure it contains pepper? The spectator sprinkles some pepper on the table-cloth. At this point you can say, "Nobody laughs when I perform, but we all have a good sneeze!" All this chatter gives you sufficient misdirection to move your right hand to the edge of the table and to drop the torn napkin into your lap. *Don't* look down when you do this—have faith! Hold your right hand loosely clenched (remember—the undamaged napkin is inside) over the table and ask the spectator to sprinkle pepper over your right fist. Then slowly open your hand and unfold the napkin, showing it to be completely restored.

This trick *isn't* easy to perform, but it's well worth the effort.

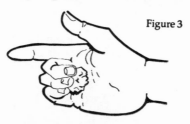

Figure 3

☛ Banana Chop

If you want a conversation stopper, this is it!

I am assuming you are going to a restaurant with some friends. Before you leave home, obtain a banana and gimmick it like this: take a needle and thread and in three places (see figure 4) guide the needle and thread under the skin of the banana (figure 5). As you can see, the thread exits through the hole it enters and if you pull the ends of the thread the banana is neatly cut without damaging the skin. Do this three times and you will have four pieces of banana inside a complete skin! Put this banana in your pocket and, when you arrive at the restaurant, have a private word with the headwaiter. Tell him you plan to perform a trick for your friends and you would be obliged if he'd help you. Point out that you will ask for a fresh banana for your dessert—would he make sure you are given *this* banana. Hand him the banana and join your friends.

At the right moment ask for a banana and, when it arrives, tell your friends you have discovered an incredible Chinese way to slice a banana. Display the banana and place it on your plate. Hold a knife about four inches above it and make three chopping movements, then say, "I think that has done it. Would somebody peel the banana for me and check to see if I have succeeded?"

Naturally, when the skin is removed, the banana is in four pieces. You may think there is a lot of preparation for what is, basically, a puzzle. I agree, but the trick is worth it. Please try it.

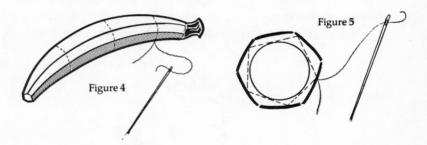

Figure 5

Figure 4

📢 Coin in Bread Roll

Another "quickie" for the dinner table.

Secretly conceal a coin in the curled fingers of your right hand. Reach for a bread roll with your left hand and place the roll on top of the coin in your right hand.

Break the roll open with both hands and push the coin upward with your right fingers. It looks as though you have discovered a coin in the very center of your roll!

📢 Miracle Taps

This is an excellent after-dinner trick: it is baffling, easy to perform, and can be repeated several times.

To perform the trick, place the following seven objects in front of you on the table:

(1) Cup	(5) Ashtray
(2) Fork	(6) Matchbox
(3) Knife	(7) Cigarette
(4) Napkin	

Ask somebody to think of any one of the seven objects. Tell him you will tap, with your pen, all the objects, and at each tap the spectator must mentally spell (to himself) one letter of the object about which he is thinking (for instance, F-O-R-K). On the last letter he must shout "Stop." You start to tap the objects, and when the spectator shouts "Stop" he finds, to his amazement, that your pen is resting on his chosen subject!

The secret is simple: The order of the objects must be memorized and objects always placed in the same order. The first two taps can be on any of the objects, and then you *must* tap the objects in the order shown in the list—the trick will work itself.

* * *

☛ Sympathetic Minds

Here is a nice trick for men who attend dinner parties with a girl friend, wife, or fiancée.

You need an envelope and a piece of paper. On the address side of the envelope write a list of names, for instance:

Linda
Pat
Lucy
Sarah
Jane

Write the same list on a piece of paper, which should be folded and placed inside the envelope.

Your other requirement is a pen. It must be the type with a slide-off cap (see figure 6). The pen is gimmicked by marking five small lines on the barrel of the pen—see illustration again. Put the pen in your inside pocket. To perform the trick, tell the audience that you and your partner have developed extremely sympathetic minds—you are *not* saying you can read each other's minds but you would like to try a little experiment that may prove interesting.

Show the envelope and the piece of paper—point out that the two lists are identical.

Ask your partner to leave the room for a moment. Tell the audience that you would like them, collectively, to choose one of the names on the list—we will assume they select "Pat." Underline this word on the sheet of paper, using your pen. Fold the paper and place it in the envelope, which should then be sealed.

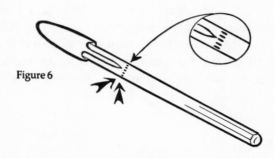

Figure 6

Now for the sneaky move. When you replace the cap on the pen, make sure that the clasp is opposite the second of the five marks on the barrel of the pen (Pat is the second name on the list). Ask your partner to return and give her the sealed envelope, which she will study with exaggerated interest. When she picks up the pen she secretly notes the mark opposite the clasp. Removing the clasp she underlines the word "Pat" on the front of the envelope. Telepathy or coincidence? Obviously the audience will realize you are coding the information in some way—this is the reason your partner studies the envelope so carefully. The pen must not, in any way, be seen to be a significant object. If you are worried about the marks on the pen, carry a duplicate pen and, when the trick is over, switch the pens. If anybody thinks the pen is suspicious, they can study it until they are blue in the face!

☞ The Baffling Bottle

In many ways this trick is not a true after-dinner trick, but the main prop (a beer bottle) is readily available in most restaurants. It is the ideal finale for a close-up routine.

You need an opaque glass bottle (a beer bottle is ideal) and a piece of rope about two feet long. Your third requirement is something audiences never see: a small hard rubber ball *just* small enough to drop into the bottle.

Prepare for the trick by concealing the rubber ball in the curled fingers of your right hand. Try to hold your hand naturally so no one will become suspicious.

To perform the trick, hand the bottle over for examination. When it is returned ask the spectators to look at the piece of rope. This gives you an opportunity to drop the rubber ball secretly into the bottle. Take the rope and insert it into the bottle. Hold the rope in position and turn the bottle upside down. Unknown to your audience, the rubber ball drops to the neck of the bottle and jams the rope. You can now release your grip on the rope and, mysteriously, it doesn't drop to the floor! (See figure 7.) You can even hold the piece of rope and let the bottle swing (figure 8). *Don't*, however, be too carefree! To end the trick, hold the bottle by its neck in your left hand. With your right hand give the rope a firm and steady tug. The ball will be pulled out and should be concealed in your left hand. The bottle and rope can be examined once again.

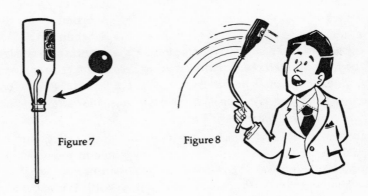

Figure 7   Figure 8

FINAL THOUGHTS

A dinner gathering usually consists of people who are friendly toward one another. Nobody will tell you to stop performing. If you feel the occasion is suitable for a few tricks, please keep your routine short—*very* short.

TRICKS
WITH
CARDS

Good card tricks will always be popular, and the person who is able to perform an entertaining routine is guaranteed an attentive audience. Although the tricks in this chapter are not difficult to perform, you must work hard to ensure your presentation is polished to perfection before showing the tricks in public.

GOLDEN RULES

Avoid tricks that are difficult to perform; amateur magicians shouldn't burden themselves with unnecessary worries. "Self-working" tricks allow you to concentrate on presentation and entertaining the audience.

Make sure your hands, nails, and shirt cuffs are spotlessly clean.

Plan your card routine very carefully, and make certain the tricks are varied. Start with a quick, dramatic trick; do not include long and complicated tricks (audiences soon get bored). The ideal length for a card routine is ten minutes, or six tricks.

Every time you perform a card routine, mentally note which tricks are well received —and which ones are not. Analyze why one trick is a success and another isn't. Improve your routine by replacing unpopular effects with new tricks, and by constantly "polishing" your favorite tricks. This never-ending search for perfection will yield handsome dividends.

Many card tricks rely on the performer's ability to **force** *or* control *a card. Forcing a card simply means giving a person an apparently free choice of any card in the pack, whereas, in reality, you force him to take a card whose identity is known to yourself. To control a card, the spectator* **does** *have a free choice of card (you don't know the identity), but the location of the card is secretly controlled by yourself, enabling you to discover its identity later on.*

The chapter starts with simple, but effective, ways to force and control a card.

☛ Forcing a Card

There are many ways to force a card. Here are three of my favorite methods:

(1) Hold the pack, face down, on the palm of your left hand. The card to be forced should be on the top of the pack—let's assume it's the three of spades. Borrow a man's handkerchief, which must be opaque, and drape it over your left hand and the deck of cards. Under cover of the handkerchief, secretly turn the pack face up. The force card will now be resting on your hand. Ask a spectator to cut the cards anywhere he wishes—remember they are still covered by the handkerchief (see figure 1). As he starts to remove the cut-off portion of the

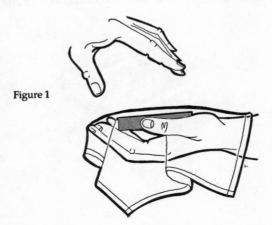

Figure 1

pack, secretly turn the cards remaining in your hand face down again. This can easily be done one-handed, under cover of the handkerchief. The top card is the three of spades once again. Tell your audience the cards have been cut in the fairest way possible; point to the top card of the deck, on your hand, and ask the spectator to remove the card of his choice. Obviously the spectators are not aware of the fact that you know the identity of this card. The information will enable you to perform some spectacular tricks.

(2) Here is a very cheeky way to force a card. The force card (three of spades again) should be on the bottom of the face-down pack. Ask a spectator to cut the cards anywhere he wishes and to place the cut-off portion of the cards face down on the table—nobody looks at the faces of the cards. Pick up the original bottom half of the deck and place it on top of, but at right angles to, the cards cut off by the spectator (see figure 2). Point out you are doing this to "mark the selected card." Continue to talk about the trick you are performing and, at the appropriate time, pick up the top half of the deck and show the face card to the spectator, asking him to remember his selected card. In reality, of course, you have shown him the original bottom card of the pack, but the complicated cutting procedure, and your patter, will have confused him into believing the card is his card. As I said earlier, this is a cheeky force, but it works!

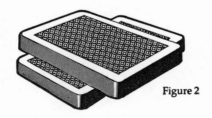

Figure 2

(3) Secretly note the tenth card from the top of the face-down pack—this is your force card.

Tell the spectator that you want him to select a card by using the science of numerology. Ask him to shout out any number between ten and twenty—we will assume he says "sixteen." Deal sixteen cards, one at a time, from the top of the deck, keeping them face down. Pick up this sixteen-card pack and tell your audience that "sixteen consists of two digits, one and six, which, when added together, total seven." Count down to the seventh card and give it to the spectator, pointing out that his card has been selected, at random, by using numbers personally chosen by him. Although it seems impossible for you to know the identity of the card, it will be the card that was originally in the tenth position! This is an extremely cunning force, which will work with any number between ten and twenty. If, for example, eighteen had been chosen, deal off eighteen cards (1 plus 8 equals 9); deal down to the ninth card, and this, again, will be the original tenth card. The tenth-card-force is a very versatile idea that can be used in many ways.

These three ways of forcing a card are simple but effective. In several card tricks, however, the spectator *can* have a free choice of card, and you find its identity later in the trick. A very good way, for example, is to ask a spectator to stab an ordinary dinner knife into the pack—the card above the knife will be used for the trick. To find the card's identity, secretly give the knife a slight twist and you will be able to see a reflection of the card's index in the polished blade of the knife.

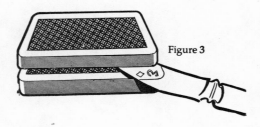

Figure 3

📌 Controlling a Card

A selected card is usually controlled by secretly placing it back into the pack next to a *locator card*. A locator card is a card whose identity is known to the performer or a card that has been altered in some way, enabling it to be easily located.

The best locator card is a *thick card*. This is simply made by *carefully* sticking a joker onto the back of any other card. You will find a thick card easy to locate. When you slide your thumb down the end of the pack, the thick card seems as stiff as a plank. To use the thick card, simply cut it to the bottom of the pack. Have a card selected and ask the spectator to place his chosen card on top of the pack. The pack should now be given a complete cut, which places the thick card above, and next to, the spectator's card. If you cut the thick card to the bottom of the pack again, the spectator's card will be on top of the pack.

📌 Wrong / Right Again

This is a splendid trick—good magic and good entertainment as well. Prepare the trick by cutting the two bottom pips off a seven of clubs (see figure 4), using a card from an old deck. This gimmicked card should be placed, out of sight, in your breast pocket, facing outward.

To present the trick, ask a spectator to select a card. Secretly force him to take the five of clubs. Tell your audience that you have a card from another pack in your top pocket—wouldn't it

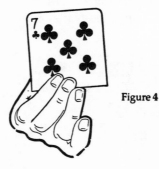

Figure 4

be an amazing coincidence if the two cards matched! *Partly* remove the gimmicked card from your pocket (take care not to expose its reduced length)—it appears to be the seven of clubs. Ask the spectator what his card is—the five of clubs. Look disappointed at your near miss, and then say, "Never mind, I *am* a magician." Remove the gimmicked card from your pocket, revealing that it only has five clubs!

This may be a simple trick, but don't underestimate its value.

☛ Double Coincidence

Here is another "coincidence" trick, and it's quite a dramatic one. The trick is simple to perform but difficult to describe. You need two decks of cards with contrasting back designs. Prepare the trick by reversing the six of spades and the four of hearts in one of the packs. Place this pack back into its box and put the box to one side. We will call this pack Pack A. Remove, from the second pack (Pack B) the six of spades and the four of hearts. Place the rest of the cards back into their box.

The trick should be performed while seated at a table. Secretly place the six of spades and the four of hearts (from Pack B) behind your knee (see figure 5). *Important:* the two cards must be facing each other, backs outward. To perform the trick, call attention to Pack A (still in its box). Tell your audience it contains 52 cards but two are more significant than the others.

Pick up Pack B and ask a spectator to give the cards a shuffle.

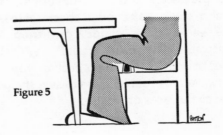

Figure 5

Take the cards back and hold them, face down, on the palm of your left hand. Tell your audience that you are going to have two cards chosen, but the choice is *not* aboveboard: in fact, it's below board, below the table! Reach under the table with your left hand, still holding Pack B. As you do so, secretly add the two cards behind your knee (the six of spades and four of hearts) to the bottom of the pack. It's easy to do so without arousing suspicion. Keeping the pack face down, on your left palm, ask the spectator to reach under the table and, without looking, cut the cards. Tell him to turn the cut-off pack of cards *face up* and place them underneath the bottom half of the pack. When this has been done, bring the pack into view and point out that the spectator cut the pack where he wished and the two cards he selected, at random, are now facing, and next to, each other somewhere in the center of the pack. Fan the cards and show the two facing cards to be the six of spades and the four of hearts. Ask another spectator to open Pack A. Two cards are reversed—the six of spades and the four of hearts!

📹 Three Stacks

Here is a neat little mystery in which you find cards chosen by three spectators.

To prepare the trick, secretly make a mental note of the top three cards of the pack. These cards are your *locator, or key, cards.*

To present the trick, ask a spectator to deal the cards, one at a time, into three face-down stacks. Unknown to the spectator or the audience the dealing places one of your locator cards on the bottom of each stack. Ask another spectator to select a card from stack one—a second spectator a card from stack two—and a third spectator a card from stack three. Each spectator must remember his card and place it back on top of the stack from which it was removed. Needless to say, the performer is not allowed to see the faces of the cards!

Each stack of cards is now given a complete cut and the first stack placed on top of the second stack and both of them placed on top of the third stack. You now have a complete pack. You can have the pack cut as many times as you wish. The spectator's cards appear to be hopelessly lost. It is, however, quite a simple matter to find the chosen cards. All you do is find your locator cards; the spectator's cards are below them. Reveal the three cards as dramatically as possible.

I think this trick lets you see how useful locator cards can be. Although the spectator's cards are freely selected and apparently lost in the pack, your locator cards follow them like bloodhounds.

☛ Face-up Revelation

I have been performing this trick for over twenty years—it's a special favorite of mine.

You need a pack of cards with an *extra* five of clubs. To prepare the trick, place one five of clubs face down on top of the pack and the other one on the bottom, *face up*.

To perform the trick, fan the cards and ask a spectator to take any one; take care not to reveal the face-up five of clubs on the bottom of the pack. Tell the audience the top card of the pack is going to do the trick for you—show it to be the five of clubs and put it on the table. Ask the spectator to place his chosen card on top of the pack, then give the cards a complete cut. Unknown to the audience, the face-up five of clubs is now above the spectator's card.

Pick up the five of clubs from the table and place it, face down, on top of the deck. Ask the spectator to stand facing the audience and to hold his hands behind his back. Hand him the cards and, as you do so, secretly turn the top card (the five of clubs) face up. Make sure this deception cannot be seen by anybody in the audience.

Ask the spectator to take the top card, the five of clubs, turn it face up and slide it into the pack anywhere he wishes. Remember, he is doing this with the cards out of sight, behind his back. Obviously the spectator actually turns the five of clubs *face down*, although he, and the audience, are not aware of this fact. Ask the spectator to show the cards and fan them face down. In the center of the pack is the five of clubs. Ask the spectator to name his chosen card and then show that the five of clubs is next to it! The trick has been done for you. At an opportune moment, put the extra five of clubs in your pocket.

☞ The Rising Card

I think you will like this mysterious trick—it is many years old but still extremely effective.

You need a pack of cards and one thick locator card, which should be on the bottom of the pack.

To perform the trick, ask a spectator to select a card and show it to the audience but not, of course, to yourself. Have the chosen card placed back on top of the pack, which is then given several cuts. The thick card should, eventually, be cut to the bottom of the pack, which places the chosen card (we will assume it's the ace of hearts) on the top again.

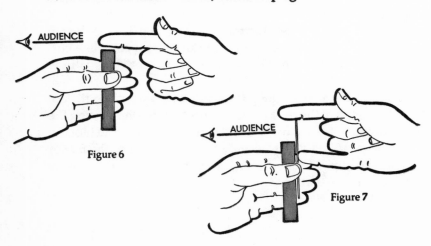

Figure 6

Figure 7

Hold the pack in your left hand, facing the audience, and rest your right forefinger on top of the cards (see figure 6). Tell the audience your forefinger is extremely sensitive and you are going to use it as a magnet to find the chosen card. Secretly extend your right little finger (see figure 7) so it touches the back of the ace of hearts; press gently and slowly move your right hand upward. Keep your left hand still. From the audience's viewpoint it looks as though your right forefinger were mysteriously attracting the chosen card.

When the ace of hearts has risen for about half its length, quickly pull it out of your left hand and show it to the spectator, asking him if it *is* his card. It is.

NOTE: Take care to ensure your audience cannot see your extended little finger—although your left hand partly covers the secret move, the trick is *not* "angle-proof" (see Deceivers' Dictionary).

☛ Behind the Back

And now for another favorite that I have been performing for over twenty years. It is quick, easy to perform, and, of course, baffling. Your only requirement is a pack of cards.

Ask a spectator to give the cards a shuffle. As you take them back, secretly glance at the bottom card of the pack—we will assume it's the jack of diamonds. Stand facing the audience and hold the cards behind your back, with the pack resting, face down, on the palm of your hand. Ask the spectator to cut the cards, anywhere he wishes, and to remove the cut-off portion of the pack, showing the face card to the audience. As he does this, secretly transfer the jack of diamonds from the bottom to the top of the cards remaining on your hand. Ask the spectator to replace his cards onto those on your hand, without letting you see the card to which he cut. Obviously his selected card is now next to the jack of diamonds, and it is a simple matter for you to fan the cards and remove the card above the jack of diamonds—it will be the spectator's card. Produce it as dramatically as you can. This is one of the few tricks that can be repeated without reducing its impact.

🖙 It's Impossible

This little trick can easily become the feature of your card routine. You need a pack of cards that has been cut in half! Take care to keep the two halves apart, otherwise you could have problems. To perform the trick, show your audience the two half-packs and have each half shuffled. Remember, keep them separated. When the first half-pack is returned, secretly make a mental note of the card at the bottom of the pack—let's say it's the jack of clubs. Force this half-card on a spectator using the handkerchief force mentioned at the beginning of the chapter. Don't reveal the card's identity, leave it face down on the table.

Pick up the other half-card pack and look through it to "see if there is a joker." This is just a ruse enabling you to position the other half-jack of clubs at the tenth position down from the top of your pack. Needless to say, the audience is not aware of your trickery. Now force the half jack of clubs using the tenth-card force described at the start of the chapter. Once again leave the half-card face down. Place the two halves together and *slowly* turn them over. They *match*—a *complete* jack of clubs.

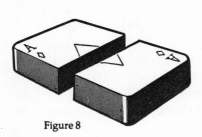

Figure 8

Figure 9

☛ In a Darkened Room (1)

Our friend the thick card enables us to perform many amazing tricks, and I think you will have a lot of fun baffling your friends with this rather spooky effect.

Tell your audience that most magicians can perform miracles in broad daylight, but only exceptional magicians can bamboozle when all the lights are out. You are an exception!

Have the cards shuffled and, when they are returned, cut the thick card to the bottom of the pack. Ask a spectator to select a card and show it to the rest of the audience (but not to you). Have it placed back on top of the pack, which is then given several cuts. Square the pack and place it on the table. Tell the audience you will now attempt to do the trick in the dark; needless to say an *extremely* difficult feat. Hold the cards, face down, on the palm of your hand and ask somebody to switch off the lights. Quickly cut the thick card to the bottom of the pack and remove the top (spectator's) card. Ask for the lights to be switched on again—slowly show the card, and enjoy hearing the gasps of amazement!

☛ In a Darkened Room (2)

Here is the perfect follow-up to the previous trick.

You need a paper bag and two identical packs of cards. Take one of the packs and carefully shorten every card by one-sixteenth of an inch (see figure 10). Use a razor-blade knife and take your time—the cards must be trimmed *neatly*. Place this short pack in your left jacket pocket (*not* in its case); the other pack is on the table. To perform the trick, pick up the pack from the table and hand it to a spectator for shuffling. Ask him to select a card and place it, out of sight, in his pocket. Ask a second spectator to do the same—and a third. Take the rest of the pack back and ask somebody to switch out the lights.

Quickly put the pack of cards in your right jacket pocket and remove the short pack from your left pocket. Grope your way toward spectator number one and ask him to replace his card into the pack. Do the same with spectators two and three. Ask for the lights to be switched on again, show the cards, and drop them into the paper bag. Ask a spectator to hold the bag tightly by its neck and give it a good shake, mixing the cards still further. Point out that three cards were selected, and returned to the pack, in total darkness—and you will now try to find the same cards even though the pack is out of sight inside the bag! Reach into the bag with both hands, and square the pack—the three selected cards are longer than the others and they can be easily located. Remove the three cards, one at a time, and ask the spectators if they are their cards. This is a *very* strong climax, even though you don't say which spectator selected each individual card. Put the pack back into your left pocket and thank your three assistants. If you are going to perform another trick, take the ordinary pack from your right pocket; nobody will notice the switch.

This trick is a reputation maker.

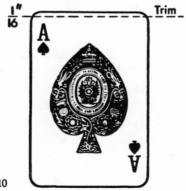

Figure 10

🖘A Tasty Dish

Tricks that are amusing, as well as amazing, always deserve a place in your routines. This good-fun card trick is popular with audiences the world over.

You need a pack of cards complete with our favorite hidden assistant—a thick card.

Have the cards shuffled; take them back and secretly cut the thick card to the bottom of the pack. Ask a spectator to select a card, look at it, and return it to the top of the pack. Give the cards several complete cuts, finally cutting the thick card to the bottom of the pack. Unknown to the audience, the chosen card is back on top of the pack again.

Ask somebody to shout out his favorite breakfast food. We will assume he says "sausages." Tell your audience you will use the freely selected word to find the freely selected card. Keeping the cards face down, start to spell the word "sausages," dealing one card into a small heap for every letter. Turn the last card face up and ask the spectator if it's his card. Look disappointed when he says it isn't. Put this last card on top of the packet of dealt-off cards. Suddenly pretend to remember that you forgot the magic word; no wonder the trick failed. Pick up the small packet of cards and place it on top of the pack; give the cards a few more cuts, ending up with the thick card on the bottom once more. Mutter "Igglybong" (a recommended magic word) and start to say "sausages" again, dealing a card for every letter. The card dealt on the last *S* will be the card chosen by the spectator—reveal it with a flourish.

The trick works with any kind of tasty breakfast dish: cornflakes, bacon and eggs, pancakes, et cetera.

Figure 11

☞ You Do As I Do

There are many versions of this splendid trick. Here is my favorite.

You need two packs of cards—one pack with red backs and the other with blue backs.

Ideally the trick should be performed while seated at a table, with a spectator opposite you.

To perform the trick, show the two packs of cards and give the blue-backed pack to the spectator—you keep the red pack. Ask the spectator to follow your movements.

First of all, each person gives his pack a shuffle, as thoroughly as he can.

Then exchange packs and give them another shuffle (you now have the blue pack; the spectator the red one).

Exchange packs again, but before you do so, secretly glance at the top card of the blue pack—this is your key card.

Remove a card from the center of the red pack. Look at it but don't show it to anybody, and place it, face down, on top of the red pack. The spectator does the same with the blue pack.

You each give your cards a complete cut and exchange packs again.

Tell the spectator to look through the pack and remove the duplicate of the card he selected earlier on from the other pack. You will do the same. However, in reality, you look through the cards and remove the card above your key card. This will be the spectator's card and it will, of course, match the card he has just removed from the cards in his hands. It appears to be a *remarkable* coincidence!

☞ Eyes in your Fingertips

It is always a good idea to start a card routine with a quick, dramatic trick. Here is an ideal opener.

You need to memorize the values of five cards. Place these

cards, in order, under your belt at the back of your trousers. Obviously the audience is not aware of this deception.

Hand the pack to be shuffled and, when it is returned, hold it behind your back. It is now a relatively simple matter to slide the cards from under your belt onto the top of the pack. Tell the audience you will see if your fingertips can reveal the identities of the cards—even though they are still behind your back! Name the top card, and show it to the audience.

You are right. Incidentally, it is good showmanship if you, too, look reasonably amazed and pleased. Name the other cards slowly and hesitantly—it all adds to the excitement.

Don't let the simplicity of this trick frighten you; it's a good effect.

Don't try to memorize more than five cards—too many would be boring.

☛ Mention My Name

Here is another good opener. In many ways it is similar to A Tasty Dish, and I therefore suggest you avoid using the two tricks in the same routine.

Once more we are using our old friend the thick card. I make no apology for the fact because I believe a thick card is one of the most subtle and effective magical gimmicks ever created.

To prepare the trick, count the total number of letters in your name—in my case, for example (Graham Reed), I total 10. To this total add 9. My personal number is, therefore, 19. Yours may be larger, or smaller; it doesn't matter either way. Place the thick card nineteenth (or whatever your total is) down from the top of the face-down pack. You are ready to perform the trick.

Cut the pack at the thick card and give a spectator the *bottom* half of the pack to shuffle. You shuffle the nineteen top cards; including the thick card, which should be kept at the bottom of the packet. Ask the spectator to select a card from his half of the pack. Take the rest of the cards back (keeping them separate from the nineteen-card packet). Ask the spectator to show his card to the rest of the audience; while he does so you turn your back—to "prevent my seeing the card," you say. This enables you to place the thick card on the bottom of the spectator's half of the pack. In one hand you now have eighteen cards—and in the other the rest of the pack (excluding the chosen card), with the thick card on the bottom. Turn around, facing the audience again, and ask the spectator to place his card, face down, on top of his half of the pack. Then place the eighteen-card packet on top of all these cards—remember, the thick card is now the bottom card of the pack. Give the cards several cuts, finally cutting the thick card to the bottom of the pack again. Tell the audience that you will use your name to find the chosen card. Spell your name, plus the word "magician," dealing one card for each letter: G R A H A M R E E D M A G I C I A N. When you say the *n* of "magician," turn the next card face up—it will be the selected card! The trick is a good opener because it introduces your name to the audience in a novel and magical way.

☞ A Stacked Pack

A *stacked pack* is a pack of cards in which the cards (unknown to the audience) have been prearranged in an order known to the performer. A stacked pack is usually used for the first trick in a routine (before the cards have been mixed). Sometimes the cards the performer has been using are secretly switched for a stacked pack.

The best way to switch an ordinary pack for a stacked pack is to have the stacked pack in your right jacket pocket. Finish your routine with the ordinary pack and place it in your left jacket pocket while your perform another trick not involving cards (and there are plenty in this book). Then remove the stacked pack from your pocket—nobody will suspect the exchange.

A simple stack is to divide the pack into two halves—all the red cards on the bottom, all the black cards on top. Obviously the audience musn't be allowed to see the faces of the cards. Using this stack we can perform quite an interesting trick.

Divide the pack into two equal halves: twenty-six cards in each, one packet all red, the other all black. Two spectators are each given half of the pack, which they shuffle—cards face down. Each spectator selects any card from his face-down packet, looks at it, and puts it in the *other* half of the pack. The two packets are placed together and given several cuts. When you look through the cards, it is obvious which ones are the chosen cards, one will be red in a packet of black cards, the other will be black in a packet of red cards. Reveal the two cards and shuffle the pack to destroy the evidence!

In my earlier book, *Magical Miracles You Can Do*, I give details of the *Eight Kings Stack*, which I strongly recommend to anybody eager to improve his or her ability with a pack of cards.

☞ The Miraculous Prediction

You need two blocks of wood, each drilled with five holes (see figure 12). The holes should be just big enough to hold a rolled piece of paper and the blocks of wood small enough to fit into a jacket pocket.

You also need ten pieces of paper. On one write *ace of hearts*; on the second *two of hearts*; and so on, to the *ten of hearts*. Carefully place one piece of paper in each hole (in an order known to yourself) and place one block of wood in your left

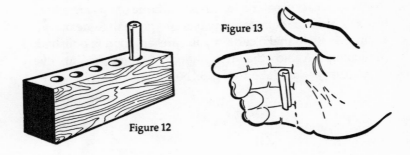

Figure 13

Figure 12

jacket pocket, the other in your right jacket pocket. You also need a stacked pack. From the top of the face-down pack, this is the sequence: AH, any card, 2H, any card, 3H, any card, 4H, any card, 5H, any card, 6H, any card, 7H, any card, 8H, any card, 9H, any card, 10H, the rest of the pack.

You also need a hat.

To perform the trick, tell the audience you had a premonition before the show started: you had a feeling that one card would be more significant than the others, and you scribbled your thoughts on a piece of paper, which is now "safely residing in this hat." Show the hat, but don't let anybody see inside. Fan the cards to show they are all different, and ask a spectator to shout out any number between one and twenty. If an odd number is called, count down and look at the card in that position; if an even number is chosen, count that number of cards and look at the *next* card. Count the cards face down and turn the selected card face up. We will assume it's the five of hearts. Casually reach into your pocket and secretly conceal the "five-of-hearts" piece of paper in the fingers of your hand (see figure 13). Reach into the hat and pretend to remove the piece of paper. Hand it to a spectator to read—the five of hearts!

FINAL THOUGHTS

Don't try to learn too many tricks. Concentrate on a few tricks that you (and your audiences) enjoy. Examine each one to see if it can be improved. Pay particular attention to ensure maximum effectiveness. Introduce one or two unusual props to give your act greater eye appeal (antique shops are a happy hunting ground for interesting bits and pieces). Rehearse your act in private to make certain your presentation is polished to perfection. Avoid the temptation to perform at every opportunity—don't be a magical bore.

MAGIC
FOR
CHILDREN

The magician who merely tries to bamboozle his audience of children will soon be in difficulties. A show for children must be colorful and lively, with plenty of audience participation.

GOLDEN RULES

When you perform for children, try not to worry about adverse comments from your audience. Boys, particularly, enjoy saying they know how tricks are done; they rarely do, but like to show off. If somebody does shout out, "I know how it's done," I suggest you smile sweetly and say, "Don't tell anybody else, it's our secret." Whatever happens, don't let youthful hecklers upset you!

Start your routine with a quick, dramatic trick. If possible, introduce an amusing magic word; mine, for example, is Igglybong.

Ask children to assist with the tricks as often as you can. Their help may be unimportant (waving a magic wand, for example), but it will give them a big thrill. Incidentally, don't ask for a volunteer—you will be buried under an avalanche of young bodies! Point to somebody and ask him or her to help you.

When children walk into the room in which your show will take place they like to see a colorful and exciting display of magical ap-

paratus. Take the trouble to arrange your props in an eye-catching way. A brightly colored tablecloth is a good start.

☛ Indian Rice Mystery

The Indian fakirs perform many mysterious tricks, and this is one of my favorites. You need a vase, shaped, if possible, like the one shown here (figure 1). The shape is important but not critical—the trick will work with differently shaped containers, even with a jam jar. You will need to experiment to make sure the trick is possible with your own container. You also need some long-grained uncooked rice and an ordinary dinner knife.

To perform the trick, show the vase and fill it with rice. Hand the knife to a spectator and ask him to stick the knife into the rice and then slowly pull it out again. Ask him to see if anything mysterious happens—it shouldn't!

Ask somebody else to try; nothing happens for him either.

Point out that you have a magic touch—and you will try to prove it. Stick the knife into the rice quickly about six or seven times. You will find the rice sinks and starts to grip the knife more and more tightly—so tightly, in fact, that you will eventually be able to stick the knife into the rice and suspend the vase in midair (see figure 2). A final tip: Try to find a knife that is large and has a broad blade which isn't too well polished. An old knife is often ideal.

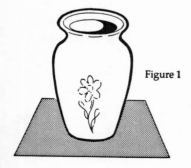

Figure 1

Figure 2

☛ The Cut-and-Restored Ribbon

We start with a trick that seems totally impossible. Imagine putting a piece of folded card around the center of a silk ribbon; the card is cut in half but the ribbon remains intact! You need a piece of half-inch-wide silk ribbon, a pair of old, blunt scissors, and a playing card. Put the playing card in a warm oven for a few moments to make it brittle.

To perform the trick, fold the playing card in half and drape the ribbon in between the two halves (see figure 3). Take the scissors and cut through the card, which will drop to the floor, in two pieces, but the ribbon is undamaged! Note: the scissors *must* be blunt and, if possible, "bow-legged."

☛ Coin through Hat

Queen Victoria probably enjoyed this trick because it's at least a hundred years old. Prepare the trick by placing a hat on a glass tumbler, and, between the two, carefully balance a quarter. About two thirds of the coin must overhang the glass; the hat will keep it in place (see figure 4). Incidentally, your audience is not aware of the coin's existence.

To perform the trick, show another quarter and say you will attempt to throw the coin into the hat and, with luck, it will magically penetrate the hat and appear in the glass.

Throw the coin, quite forcefully, into the hat, trying to strike the inside of the hat on the opposite side from the hidden coin. This will dislodge the coin, which will drop into the glass,

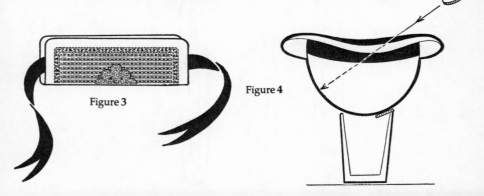

Figure 3

Figure 4

creating the illusion that the coin penetrated the crown of the hat!

Pick up the hat and display the coin in the glass. Keep the coin in the hat concealed beneath your fingers.

☞ Afghan Bands

For a combination of amusement and amazement, this trick takes a lot of beating. You need three strips of paper about four feet long, two inches wide. The ends are glued together to form large loops. Although the loops appear identical, they have been gimmicked in a rather subtle manner, and each one is different from the others. As you will see in figure 5, loop *A* is free from deception. The ends of loop *B*, however, are given a twist before they are glued together. The ends of loop *C* are given *two* twists before gluing.

Keep the loops separate and remember which is which.

To perform the trick, show loop *A* and, with a pair of scissors, cut the loop lengthwise along its circumference. You will end up with two loops—what everybody expects.

Pick up loop *B* and cut it in a similar manner—say a magic word or two as you do so—and you will be amazed (your audience will be too) to see, not two loops, but one double-sized loop!

Loop *C*, when cut, will produce two loops—but linked together! The trick is visually startling—*ideal* for children.

Figure 5

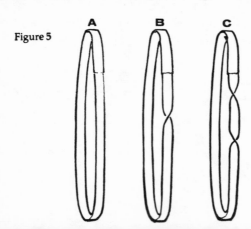

☛ Card on Racket

This is one of the few card tricks suitable for a large audience of children. It is easy to do and very spectacular. You need a table-tennis racket, which must have an identical front and back—an all-wooden racket is ideal. You also want a pack of alphabet cards and a roll of double-sided tape.

Prepare the trick by putting two strips of double-sided tape on the back of a letter *A*. Remove the backing to expose the sticky surface of the tape (see figure 6). Place this card face down on a table behind some other prop. You also need the ability to force a card (see Chapter 4). Force another letter *A* on a spectator. Ask him to show it to the rest of the audience and replace the card in the pack, which can be thoroughly shuffled. Show the racket, both sides, and place it down on the table *on top of the prepared letter* A. Ask your assistant to hold the pack of cards and, when you give the word, to throw the cards toward you. Pick up the racket (the card will adhere to the back) and hold it in your right hand. Keep the card on the back, out of sight. Ask for the cards to be thrown and hit them, forcefully, with the racket and, as you do so, turn the bat around to expose the card fastened to it. See figure 7. The trick is visually perfect—it really *does* look as though you had caught the chosen card on the racket.

NOTE: When you hit the pack with the racket, move the racket *quickly* to provide cover for the turn-over movement.

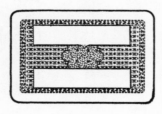

Figure 6

Figure 7

☛ Rising Pencil

Another trick that is as effective today as when it was first invented.

You need a long wooden pencil, a beer bottle, and about two feet of very thin fishing line. Secure one end of the fishing line to the blunt end of the pencil and the other end of the fishing line to a shirt button about six inches above the top of your trousers. Put the pencil in your inside jacket pocket, taking care not to break or tangle the line. Put the bottle on a table.

To perform the trick, show the bottle and hold it close to your body at about chest height. Remove the pencil from your pocket and drop it, blunt end first, into the bottle. The fishing line, at this point, should be slack, allowing the pencil to move quite freely.

Holding the bottle in your left hand, start to move it away from your body. At the same time wave your right hand in a mysterious way and mutter a few magic words. The fishing line will become taut and the pencil will rise into the air (see figure 8). By moving the bottle closer to, or farther from, your body, the rise and fall of the pencil can be easily controlled. The bottle can even be sealed if you make a gimmicked cork (see figure 9).

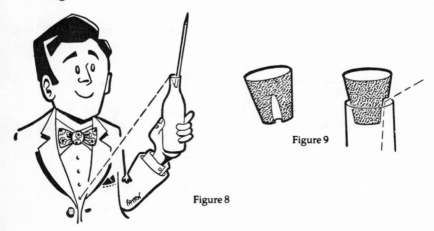

Figure 9

Figure 8

📣 Magic Welding

This is an easy-to-do version of a magical classic. It is a splendid trick for children.

You need twenty key rings about 1½ inches in diameter. Link ten of the rings together to form a short chain. You also need a piece of half-inch-diameter dowel rod—this is your magic wand. Your third requirement is a glass tumbler.

Prepare the trick by folding the chain, concertina fashion, and slide it onto one end of the magic wand (see figure 10). Put the loose links in the tumbler. Everything should be placed on a table, with the wand out of sight behind a crumpled handkerchief or another prop.

To perform the trick, show the wand, keeping the chain concealed from view under your hand. Pick up the tumbler with your other hand and ask two or three people to remove the loose links and slide them onto the wand—make sure you keep the chain hidden. Leave the tumbler with a spectator.

Turn to the table and, as you do so, transfer the wand from one hand to the other. This very natural movement enables you to cover the *loose* links and reveal the chain which, however, appears to be loose links: the fact they are linked together is not apparent.

Ask for the tumbler and slide the bunched chain off the wand into the tumbler. Put the wand, plus the loose links, behind some other object on your table. Rattle the chain in the tumbler, to cover any noise the loose links may make.

Move toward your audience shaking the tumbler. Wave your wand and say, "Girls and boys, the links have magically joined together—*look*." Throw the chain into the air, catch it, and display it between both hands. The end of a superb trick.

Figure 10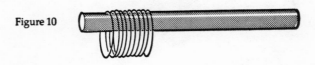

✒A Stitch in Time

This trick introduces you to a versatile magical prop, which can
be used for a wide variety of effects. A flat changing bag can
easily be made from any spare piece of material—it is simply a
small bag about ten inches square (see figure 11) with a secret
center partition that divides the bag into two compartments.
Any small item, placed in one compartment, can easily be
exchanged for a similar article in the other compartment,
without the audience's knowledge. For example, a red handkerchief can be changed into a blue one; single pieces of rope
join together; a message will appear on a blank piece of paper.
The possibilities are limited only by your imagination.

We will use the changing bag for an effective trick in which a
button is "magically" stitched onto a piece of cloth.

Apart from the changing bag, you need two identical pieces
of cloth about four inches square, two large matching buttons,
and a ball of orange wool.

Prepare the trick by stitching one of the buttons (use the
orange wool) onto the center of one of the pieces of material.
Place this piece of cloth into compartment A of the changing
bag. The other piece of cloth, the loose button, and about ten
inches of wool should be on a table.

To perform the trick, hold the bag and turn it inside out,
showing compartment B. The bag seems to be completely
empty. Turn the bag right side out again—hold it in your left
hand and keep compartment A shut.

Figure 11

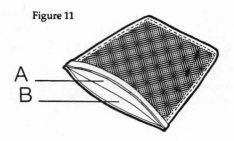

A

B

Show the piece of material, the button, and the wool, and drop them all into compartment B. Give the bag a shake with both hands; as you do so, close the opening to compartment B and hold it shut between the fingers and thumb of your left hand. Compartment A is now open.

Wave your hand over the bag and say a few "magic sewing words." Reach into the bag and show that the button is now stitched onto the piece of material. Turn the bag inside out and show it is empty again—this should convince any skeptics in the audience!

☛ Flying Money

This is another effective trick for children. It's easy to do, the props are inexpensive, and it's a lot of fun.

You need a dollar bill, a large handkerchief, a few small rubber bands, a clear plastic tumbler from which the bottom has been removed, and a silk scarf.

You also need a piece of blank paper the same size as the dollar bill. Prepare the trick by folding this piece of paper in half lengthwise, and then rolling it up into a tight little bundle: Secure it with a rubber band. Slip this bundle into the hem of the handkerchief near a corner. Place everything on a table, and you are ready to perform the trick.

Tell the audience you are going to show them an amazing trick with one of your favorite toys—show the dollar bill.

Ask for two volunteers. We'll assume one is a boy, the other a girl. Show the tumbler to be empty by holding it sideways to the audience and throwing it in the air. The fact that it is bottomless will not be noticed. Cover it with the scarf and snap a rubber band around the mouth of the tumbler to keep the scarf in position. Ask the girl to hold the covered tumbler, upright, between her two hands. Show the dollar bill again and have somebody initial it; roll it up (as you did with the piece of paper) and secure it with a rubber band.

Hold the dollar bill in your left fingertips and pick up the handkerchief by the corner in which the rolled piece of paper is concealed—hold the handkerchief in your left hand. Now for the important move. Cover your left hand with the handkerchief and ask the boy if he can feel the dollar bill through the thickness of the handkerchief—make sure, however, he holds the rolled piece of paper. Ask him to keep a tight grip and remove your hand, keeping the dollar concealed in your curled fingers.

Ask the girl for the tumbler and place it on your left hand. The tumbler is bottomless, so the bill goes inside. All this is, of course, covered by the scarf—the audience is unaware of the deception that is taking place.

Give the audience a quick recap: "Girls and boys. An empty glass tumbler which Ann has carefully guarded for me, and a dollar bill, which, I hope, Timothy has—but miracles still happen—WATCH!" As you shout "Watch," pull the handkerchief from Timothy's grasp—the bill has vanished! Ask Ann to take the scarf off the tumbler and then jerk your hand upwards to shoot the note into the air. Have the initials checked—it's the same note!

☞ The Indestructible Napkin

"Torn and Restored" tricks are always popular with young audiences, and this one has an extra punch.

You need three paper napkins.

Before you start the trick (unknown to the audience) roll two of them into tight balls, which are concealed in the curled fingers of your right hand (see figure 12).

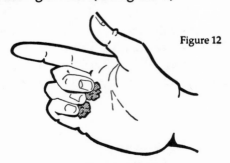

Figure 12

Show the other napkin and tear it into several small pieces, which you then squeeze into a ball. As you do this, secretly exchange the torn pieces for one of the complete napkins concealed in your hand.

Say a magic word and open the napkin to show it is restored—at the same time drop the other complete napkin to the floor. Needless to say, the audience will shout out, thinking they have discovered how the trick works.

Look crestfallen as you glance at the napkin on the floor—crumple up the napkin in your hand and, with it, the torn pieces. Put them into your pocket as you pick the napkin off the floor. "Girls and boys. You spotted how the trick works, but a *true* magician can always work miracles." Open the napkin and show that it, too, has been restored!

☞ Just Chance

This is rather a novel trick, and I think even very experienced performers will find it of interest.

You need three small, baby-sized rubber boots—one red, one yellow, and one green. They can be obtained from most large department stores. You also need three large clips, three envelopes, and three $5 bills, plus a supply of candies (in wrappers), and a pair of scissors.

To prepare the trick, clip an envelope to the front of each boot (see figure 13). Fold each $5 bill into quarters and clip a bill on the *inside* of each boot (see figure 14). The audience is unaware of these bills, and they must be kept from their view. Finally drop a few candies into each boot. To perform the trick, tell your audience you would like to show them your lucky

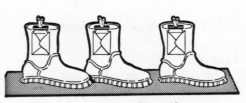

Figure 13

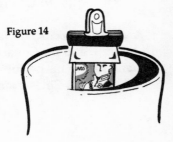

Figure 14

boots. Point out that one, and only one, of the envelopes contains something of value—the other two are empty.

Ask a boy to choose one of the three colors—red, yellow, or green. Go to the boot of his choice and open, and remove, the clip (the $5 bill will drop down into the boot). Remove the envelope and give it to the boy to hold. Ask a girl to select another color and follow the same procedure—remove the clip and give her the envelope to hold.

You are left with the third boot. Tell your audience this envelope is yours. Stand behind the boot and place your left fingers, at the front, on the envelope and your left thumb, inside the boot, on the $5 bill. With your right hand unfasten the clip and slide the envelope upward, in your left hand, with the $5 note out of sight behind it still held by your left thumb.

Ask the girl and boy to look inside their envelopes and, as they do so, snip the top end off your envelope with the pair of scissors held in your right hand.

Grip the envelope in your right hand and pull your left hand upward. The $5 bill will appear to come from within the envelope—a deceptive move.

Needless to say, the boy and girl will find their envelopes to be empty, and they should be given some candies, from the appropriate boot, as a consolation prize. Take care *not* to give them one of the $5 bills by mistake!

The colors red, yellow, and green are suggested for the boots to give the trick a "safety first" theme. You could say, "the trick is a gamble, and nobody should gamble with his life"— remind the children what the three colors stand for.

☛ Squared Circle

A colorful production is a splendid way to finish a show for children, and the Squared Circle is an easy-to-make trick that many magicians perform with success.

A Squared Circle production box consists of three parts.

Figure 15

Firstly, there is the load container, which is a large tin can covered with dull black material (see figure 15).

Secondly, you need a colorful bottomless cylindrical tube, which is a *loose* fit over the load container and about two inches taller.

Finally you need the outer, square container, which is also bottomless. It has several openings at the front, enabling audiences to see inside. The interior of this container is painted a dull, matt black.

Prepare the trick by filling the load container with as many silk scarves as you can—the more, the merrier!

The load container goes inside the tube, and both tubes go inside the outer square container.

To perform the trick, pick up the square container and show it to be empty—allow the audience to see through it from all angles. Place the container back over the tubes (open front facing audience) and remove the bottomless tube and show it to be empty, too.

Although the load container is now visible through the openings in the square its dull black color makes it appear to be the interior of the outer container—an effective bit of camouflage. Place the round tube back into position, taking care not to catch the load container as you do so.

From the audience's viewpoint the two visible containers have been convincingly shown empty, and the fact that you can now produce a seemingly endless supply of silk scarves from their interior tube is, to say the least, quite astounding.

FINAL THOUGHTS

If you perform for young children, remember that they want to be entertained. Select simple, direct tricks, with the opportunity for audience participation, if possible. Keep your routines short; audiences soon get bored. It is said that the worst entertainer ever seen was a Chinese performer called On Too Long!

MAGICAL
MIRACLES FOR
ROMANTIC MOMENTS

The ability to perform a few conjuring tricks is a useful asset when you are entertaining a friend of the opposite sex. It is all too easy for conversation to become stilted, and a quick trick or two can be a welcome ice breaker. Some tricks are designed to make you the center of attraction at parties; others are for more intimate moments.

GOLDEN RULE

Avoid doing too many tricks in one session.

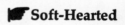

Figure 1

Soft-Hearted

Here is a nice quick trick that is ideal for intimate moments when you are sitting in a quiet place with your special girl. It may not be the world's greatest mystery, but its romantic message appeals to most people.

To prepare the trick, obtain a large nylon foam sponge and carefully cut three hearts about 2 inches across (see figure 1). Try to make them all as similar as possible. Put all three hearts into your right jacket pocket.

To present the trick, remove one heart from your pocket and

65

place it on your left hand, which should be held palm up. With your right hand reach into your jacket pocket again and palm the second heart in your curled fingers—the third heart is openly displayed between thumb and forefinger (see figure 2). Place the visible heart on your left palm with the other one; keep your right fingers curled to conceal the heart of which your girl friend is unaware. Ask her which of the two hearts she prefers. When she points to one, reach for it with your right hand and pick it up, at the same time squeezing the concealed heart against it (see figure 3). The two hearts will squash together and look like one. Keep squeezing the two hearts and press them into your friend's palm and, using your left hand, bend her fingers over the hearts, so they are covered at all times by your fingers or hers. Ask her to keep her hand tightly clenched over the heart/s. Remember she is aware of only *one* heart in her hand. Show the remaining heart and put it into your pocket. Tell your friend that you will now say a magic word and the heart will jump from your pocket into her hand with the other one. Mutter "Igglybong" a few times and ask her to open her hand—*two* hearts! You might want to say that it's right for two hearts to be together.

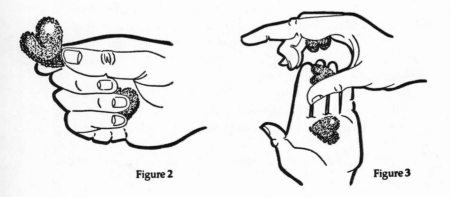

Figure 2   Figure 3

☞ Love Diviner

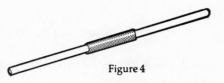

Figure 4

The following trick is another old friend that you will enjoy performing. Incidentally, another version appears elsewhere in the "Impromptu Tricks" chapter. You need two plastic rods, about 1½ inches long and ¼ inch in diameter. I made mine from a knitting needle. To prepare the trick, slide a ¾ inch length of rubber tubing over the ends of the rods—the rubber must fit tightly (see figure 4). You will find that if you pull them together and hold them between thumb and forefinger (figure 5), the rods look quite normal. If you release the pressure of your thumb, the rods fly apart in a startling manner (see figure 6). The rods can be placed together again and, if you tug hard, they can be pulled out of the rubber tubing, which can be secretly dropped on the floor. Everything can now be examined without danger of the secret's being revealed.

There are many ways to use this little device, but for the purpose of romance I suggest you show the two rods to your girl friend (keeping the rubber tubing covered). Tell her the rods are, literally, divining rods, but instead of locating water they react when they are close to somebody who would be the ideal partner for yourself. Ask her to hold out her hand. Hold the rods above her palm, release your grip slightly, and—instant reaction. If this fails to impress your lady, give up—nothing will succeed!

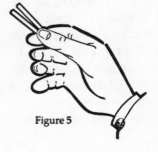

Figure 5   Figure 6

☛ Telephone Mind Reading

If you have a good friend willing to assist you and a girl friend you wish to impress, this is *the* trick for you. Once again the effect is amazing, and the method simple.

To prepare the trick, have the following list typed—you need a copy in your phone book and your friend needs another copy close to his telephone.

Ace—Roger	
Two—Tom	
Three—Bill	
Four—Ian	
Five—Henry	CLUBS—*Brown*
Six—Hugh	HEARTS—*White*
Seven—Mike	SPADES—*Black*
Eight—Timothy	DIAMONDS—*Green*
Nine—Simon	
Ten—Mark	
Jack—Alan	
Queen—Peter	Your friend's telephone
King—Ron	number ....

To present the trick, ask your friend to shuffle a pack of cards and spread them, face up, on a table. Then ask her to throw a coin onto the cards—the card on which the coin falls will be her chosen card. A perfectly free and random selection, which you couldn't possibly have influenced. We will assume it's the jack of diamonds. Tell her you have a friend who can read minds—over the telephone! Remove your phone book, ostensibly to check your friend's telephone number, and secretly glance at the name opposite Jack (for jack of diamonds). It's Alan. The code for diamonds is green, so you simply tell your friend to phone Alan Green (and ask for him by name) and ask him if he can read her mind and tell her the identity of her chosen card. Obviously as soon as your friend hears the name Alan Green, he quickly glances at his list, decodes the name, and says he is getting the impression of a red card—a high-value card—is it the jack of diamonds? Another triumph!

☛ Pulse Reading

I have performed this trick more times than I care to remember. It is suitable for parties, but can also be performed for just one person, especially a member of the opposite sex.

All you need is a pack of cards and some acting ability.

To present the trick, ask your girl friend to shuffle the cards and return them to you when they have been thoroughly mixed. Secretly glimpse the bottom card of the pack; we will assume it's the three of spades. Force this card (see "Tricks with Cards") on your friend and have the card returned to the pack. Ask her to give the cards another shuffle. Take the pack and spread the cards face up on a tabletop—secretly noting the location of the three of spades.

Tell your friend the trick is based on the fact that "our pulses beat quicker at certain times"—and you are going to try and find her card by "reading" her pulse reaction.

Ask her to extend her left forefinger and hold her wrist with your right hand, fingers underneath on her pulse (see figure 7). Start to move her hand over the cards, giving a commentary as you do so. "You have a very positive pulse beat, a sign of an active, healthy, life . . . I think the trick should work . . . no reaction so far . . . just a slight quickening . . . we must be getting close. Yes a *very* strong reaction—am I right; is it *this* card—the three of spades?"

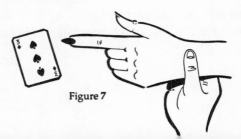

Figure 7

🏳A Subtle Hint

I think this trick will appeal to readers with a romantic mind.

You need a pack of cards (plus joker). Discard all the red cards *except* the queen of hearts.

To perform the trick, ask your girl friend to mix the cards, keeping them face down. Do *not* let her see the faces of the cards. Take the cards back and look through them on the pretext of removing the joker. While doing so, secretly make sure the queen of hearts is the tenth card from the top (or left of the cards as you look at them).

Place the packet of cards face down on the table. Unknown to your audience, the tenth card down is the queen of hearts. Point out that she shuffled the cards, and the trick is now out of your control and in the hands of fate. Ask her to think of any number she likes between ten and twenty. Stress that she has a completely free choice—although destiny may be guiding her!

We will assume she says nineteen. Pick up the packet of cards, keeping them face down, and slowly deal, off the top, nineteen face-down cards. Put the remaining cards on the table. Pick up the nineteen-card packet and point out that "nineteen consists of two digits, one and nine, which, when added together, total ten."

Count down to the tenth card and turn it face up—the queen of hearts. Tell your friend this may not seem remarkable, but destiny and fate have persuaded her to select the only red card in the packet. Turn all the other cards face up for a dramatic climax.

The trick will work whatever number is chosen—just add the two digits together and count down to the appropriate card.

Needless to say, you have a splendid opportunity to tell your girl friend that she, alone, is your queen of hearts.

☛ Handwriting Analysis

Here is a superb trick, and I ask you to treat it with great respect. I have used it for many years, and it still continues to be one of the favorite items in my close-up repertoire. It is ideal for parties, and it is especially effective if it is presented as an experiment in graphology—*not* as a conjuring trick. Skill is not required, but you *do* need to be a quick thinker.

To prepare the trick, obtain a number of postcards and have the words PLEASE WRITE ON THIS SIDE typed at the top of the blank side on each card. I have had a rubber stamp made, which is worth consideration if you, too, find the trick to be popular with audiences.

Now for the deception. On the first card, carefully put a minute pencil dot above the *P* of PLEASE. On the second card, a small dot above the *L;* on the third card, above the *E,* and so on. Unknown to your audience, the cards are now marked. Place them in your pocket, making sure you do not alter their order.

To perform the trick, tell the people in your audience that you have been studying, in great depth, the science of graphology, and you believe you can demonstrate the way in which a person's character is revealed by his handwriting.

Remove the cards from your pocket and give the first card to a person on your extreme left. Distribute the rest of the cards (limit yourself to eight cards maximum) from left to right, moving clockwise around the room. The first card should be with a spectator on your extreme left and the last card with somebody on your extreme right. Do not give cards to people you know very well.

Figure 8

Ask each person participating to write anything he likes on his card, while you turn your back or leave the room. Ask another spectator to collect the cards, mix them, and return them to you. You are now at the point where you need to be a quick thinker! A glance at the first card will reveal its mark, which, in turn, tells you which spectator wrote on that particular card. For example, a pencil dot above the L indicates it was the second person.

Look at the words written on the card and the style of writing, and start to make a few appropriate comments. "This appears to be the writing of a woman—and I suspect a woman with a warm sense of humor. The strong capital letters tell me she is also very kind, and the rounded vowels lead me to believe she is a neat and tidy person. Joan—am I right in thinking this is *your* writing?" Hand the card back and wait for confirmation that you have divined correctly.

Work your way through the rest of the cards, making comments that are kindly, though rather vague. A glance at each spectator, in turn, is often extremely fruitful; most people's characters are revealed by their clothes and general bearing. Look for clues: engagement rings, the person's manner of dress, et cetera. Avoid being too specific. It would be wrong, for example, to say, "I think this person has just become engaged." How much nicer to say "The flourishes in this person's writing suggest she is enjoying a particularly happy time at the moment—and romance is in the air." The horoscopes in your daily newspaper will provide many useful phrases. Another word of warning: Do *not* make any predictions for the future; concentrate on divining character.

As I said before, this really is a superb trick. It is different every time you perform it. You *do* need an alert mind. Present it as a serious, scientific exercise, and people will believe you are a very gifted person.

☞ Mind Reader's Rod

Here is another of my personal favorites, which I think you, too, will find a lot of fun. At the end of the trick most audiences are so amazed they sit in stunned silence. Don't, therefore, be upset if you fail to receive any applause.

In common with many good tricks, the secret is very simple, but assuming the trick is well presented, with a touch of showmanship, the effect is extremely dramatic.

To prepare the trick, find an old pack of cards and cut the ten of clubs in half across its width. This half-card is your secret gimmick. You also need a small piece of Plexiglas rod about one inch in diameter and three inches long. If you cannot find a suitable rod, a large glass marble is just as good. Place the half-card gimmick in your right jacket pocket (facing your body); the rod is also placed in the same pocket. A pack of cards is the final requirement.

To present the trick, ask a man to join you and seat him on a chair facing the audience. Choose somebody who is friendly but *not* the "life and soul of the party." Tell him he has been chosen because you believe he has a perceptive brain; he may even be capable of reading other people's minds.

Ask him to give the cards a shuffle and return them to you when he is satisfied they are well mixed. Fan the cards toward yourself, ostensibly to remove the joker, and secretly transfer the ten of clubs to the top of the pack. Approach your favorite lady in the audience and force the ten of clubs on her (see "Tricks with Cards"). Obviously she believes she has had a free and random choice. Ask her to look at the card, remember it, but *not* show it to anybody else.

Tell the audience you have selected two assistants very carefully; they both have a high sense of perception and clarity of mind—attributes that are essential if the trick is to succeed.

Put the cards on the table and reach into your pocket for the mind reader's rod, which should be held between the right thumb and forefinger. While removing the rod, secretly palm the half-card gimmick (see figure 9). *At all times*, keep the back of your hand toward the audience to ensure they cannot see the gimmick.

Tell your audience the rod is a meeting point for the two minds involved in the experiment. Ask the woman to look intently at the rod and think, all the time, about her chosen card. Stand on the right of your seated male assistant and ask him to look at the rod but *not* to say anything. He will see the rod *and* the gimmick—the view shown in figure 9. After a moment or two, ask him if he is getting the impression of a card. If he says yes, ask what the card is. Hopefully he will have realized that he has just been recruited as an instant confederate and will enter into the fun by naming the half-card—the ten of clubs! Ask the woman what card she is thinking about—the ten of clubs! Put the rod and gimmick into your pocket and thank your two assistants for their help.

There are several good tricks that depend on instant confederates, and it is worth stressing that the careful selection of a suitable person is *all*-important. As I said earlier, avoid the "life and soul of the party." This type of person can sometimes be jealous of the amount of attention you are getting and may deliberately ruin your trick to try and get a few laughs for himself—I've seen it happen! I suggest you choose a man who is pleasantly friendly and not too shy.

Figure 9

☛ Oversensitive

This very old trick is strongly recommended as a good party stunt.

You need a piece of paper about ten inches square.

To perform the trick, tell your audience it is possible for concentrated thought waves to travel from one mind to another. You are not saying mind reading is possible—only that a strong mind is capable of transferring an impulse to another receptive mind. Point out that you are feeling very receptive, and you feel sure the members of your audience are all strong-minded.

Take the sheet of paper and tear it into nine pieces (see figure 10).

Select nine spectators and give a piece of paper to each person, making certain you mentally note who receives the center piece of paper. As you will see in figure 10, this piece of paper is "marked" in a subtle way: whereas all the other pieces have one or two straight edges, the center piece is torn on all four sides. We will call the spectator who has this piece of paper X. Ask X to write, on his piece of paper, the initials of a woman. It may be a friend or a famous personality. Nobody should see what he has written. The piece of paper is to be folded when he has finished. The other spectators are asked to write the initials of men. Once again they do so privately, and then fold their pieces of paper.

Figure 10

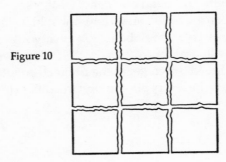

Tell your audience that you have developed a remarkable sensitivity, which enables you to tell which is the piece of paper with female initials on it. All the pieces of paper should be collected, mixed, and placed on a tabletop.

With a look of concentration, start to pick up the pieces of paper, open them, and mumble, under your breath, the various initials. The female initials are obvious from the shape of the piece of paper on which they are written. Pick up one of the male initials, read it aloud, saying "F.B., without doubt a man," crumble the piece of paper and put it into an ashtray. Do the same with another male initial, and another, until you only have the female initials left. "Ladies and Gentlemen," you say, "I will stake my reputation on the fact that these initials—L.S., belong to a woman. Will the writer please confirm whether I'm right or wrong?" Obviously you are right.

Incidentally, I usually set fire to the pieces of paper, conveniently destroying all incriminating evidence!

☛ Ring on Ribbon

Here is a startling trick that is ideal for close-up performances.

You need a large, opaque handkerchief, a piece of ribbon 30 inches long and half an inch wide, a solid metal ring about one inch in diameter, and a safety pin.

To perform the trick, spread the ribbon across a tabletop and tell your audience to watch closely. Lay the ring on the center of the ribbon. (See figure 11.) Cover the center of the ribbon, and the ring, with the handkerchief. Tell the spectators the ends of the ribbon are in full view, and it would be impossible for the ring to penetrate the ribbon. However, you are a magician and you will attempt to "magish!" Under cover of the handkerchief, thread the center of the ribbon through the ring (figure 12). Fasten the safety pin through the ribbon (figure 13).

Firmly press your right forefinger through the loop at point X onto the table. With your left hand, pull the left-hand end of the ribbon to your left. Unknown to your audience, this will thread the ribbon through the ring. (Don't move your right forefinger until the movement is completed.) Display the ribbon between your two hands and ask somebody to remove the safety pin. The ring spins happily on the ribbon!

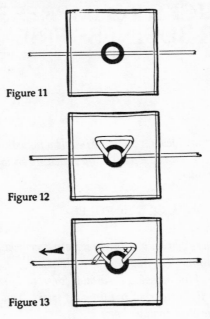

Figure 11

Figure 12

Figure 13

FINAL THOUGHTS

"Magical Miracles for Romantic Moments" is perhaps a unique chapter in the history of conjuring books. I would like to add that I write from experience—it was thanks to magic I met the girl who is now my wife.

IMPROMPTU
TRICKS TO IMPRESS
YOUR BUSINESS FRIENDS

The following tricks are ideal for business people who want to add a bit of zest to a coffee break, an office party, or an evening socializing with colleagues and customers.

GOLDEN RULES

Do not perform unless you are absolutely certain everybody wants you to do so. Even assuming the audience is enthusiastic, use your own judgment to decide if the occasion is suitable for your talents.

Avoid too many light-hearted and flippant tricks. You don't want to be remembered as an amusing clown.

Choose tricks and props in keeping with your age. Many tricks look distinctly childish.

Make sure you treat people who help you with courtesy and tact. Being an entertainer does not give you the right to embarrass anybody in your audience. Apart from not being very nice, it's not very sensible in business surroundings.

It must be said again: Don't overstay your welcome.

☛ Time Prediction

This is a magnificent trick, which is ideal for those occasions when you are dining with business colleagues. The effect is mind-boggling! I'm fully aware that the method sounds too simple to work, but please give the trick a trial and I think you, too, will become a fan. The effect is very direct. While relaxing over after-dinner coffee with a few business associates, the conversation turns to mind reading and magic. Casually you mention that you would like to try a little experiment that may, or may not, work. Calling the headwaiter to your table, you hand him your watch with the request that he take it away, reset it to any time he likes, and bring it back in a minute or two. While he is away you scribble on a piece of paper— "8:20." When the headwaiter returns he has set the watch to—8:20!

The secret *is* simple. Before dinner, have a quiet, private word with the headwaiter and tell him you intend showing a conjuring trick to your friends. Tell him the trick's plot and ask him if he will kindly help you by setting the watch to 8:20. You should have a willing partner in crime! *Please* don't avoid this trick because it makes use of a stooge—it is one of the most effective tricks I have ever encountered.

☛ The Gambling Man

Now for a splendid card trick. Only twelve cards are used, and they can easily be carried in your wallet. To perform the trick, you need an audience of at least two people.

Unknown to the spectators, the twelve cards are stacked. From the top of the face-down packet, this is the sequence:

Any red card, 2 black cards, 2 red cards, 2 black cards, 2 red cards, 2 black cards, any red card.

To perform the trick, hold the pack of cards in your left hand in the dealing position—keep them face down.

Tell the audience that you have a pack of cards with several pairs of cards, each pair consisting of a red card and a black card.

With your left thumb, push off the top two cards (don't alter their relative positions), and show them to a spectator on your left, saying, "A red card and a black card." Place the two cards face down on the table. Push off the next two cards (once again don't alter their order) and show them to a spectator on your right, saying, "A red card and a black card." Place the cards on top of the other two on the table (face down). Continue this pattern (two off the top—shown to alternate spectators— placed on top of the other cards on the table), until you have no more cards.

Pick up the packet of cards and remind the spectators that they have seen several pairs of red/black cards. Casually pick up the top card and gesture with it as you tell the story about a reformed card cheat who taught you a secret way to alter the order of a pack of playing cards—make this story as interesting as you can, and while you have the audience's attention put the "top" card on the *bottom* of the face-down packet. Don't look at the cards as you do this and nobody will suspect anything.

Hold the cards in your left hand and give them a squeeze with your right hand—explain that this is the "secret" move. To prove you have succeeded, turn the top two cards over. They are both red. The next two are both black. Then two more reds, and so it goes on. It looks as though you had altered the sequence of all twelve cards—an incredible climax. Warning —this is the type of trick that will reduce your invitations to bridge parties!

☛ Tees for Two

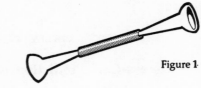

Figure 1

Here is the perfect follow-up to the Gambling Man. The two tricks blend together to form an impressive five-minute routine. You need the twelve cards used in the previous trick and two golf tees that have been gimmicked by sticking their pointed ends into a small piece of rubber tubing (see figure 1).

If the two tees are held together, the rubber tubing cannot be seen (figure 2) and the tees look quite ordinary. If, however, you release the pressure of your thumb, the tees will spring apart in a very startling manner—(see figure 3).

To perform the trick, have the cards shuffled and ask a spectator to select one. Secretly note the bottom card of the packet (this is your key card). Have the chosen card placed back on top of the pack, which should be given several cuts. Deal all the twelve cards face up. The card that follows your key card will be the spectator's card. If your key card is the last one dealt, the spectator's card was the first one off the top of the pack.

Spread the cards over a tabletop and show the golf tees. Hold them as shown in the second illustration, concealing the rubber tubing. Tell your audience the tees will react when they locate the chosen card. Move the tees over the cards and release the pressure of your thumb when the tees are above the spectator's card—they will fly apart. Ask the spectator if it *is* his card. While he is confirming you are correct, slide the tees out of the rubber tubing, which can be dropped on the floor. The tees can be thrown on the table for examination.

You will find another version of this trick in the "Magical Miracles for Romantic Moments" chapter.

Figure 2

Figure 3

☞ Business-Card Prediction

An *ideal* trick for business people. You need a packet of twenty business cards, all facing the same way (name-and-address side upward). On the back of the tenth card down write the words: YOU WILL CHOOSE THIS CARD.

To perform the trick, show the packet of cards and ask somebody to choose any number between 10 and 20. We will assume it's 13. Count off thirteen cards (place the rest of the visiting cards to one side). Pick up the thirteen-card packet and say, "Thirteen consists of two digits, one and three, which, when added together, equal four." Count down to the fourth card and show the message on its reverse side—it appears as though you had correctly predicted the spectator's choice.

The trick works with any number providing the prediction card is tenth from the top. For example, let's suppose eighteen had been chosen—count off eighteen cards (1 + 8 = 9), then count down to the ninth card, which, again, will be the prediction card.

☞ Doodle Analysis

This is the perfect partner to the previous trick. I have performed it scores of times and it has never let me down. You need six business cards. Each one is marked with a tiny pencil dot above one of the letters on the card. The first card has a dot above the first letter, the second card a dot above the second letter, and so on (see figure 4), with dots enlarged for clarity).

Keep the six cards in order. I carry mine in a special pocket in my wallet.

Tell your audience that most business people doodle on their scrap pads, and these doodles can reveal a lot about the doodler's personality. In fact, many large companies have scrap pads shredded to prevent competitive organizations from gaining secret information from doodles!

Tell your audience that you would like to try some applied psychology to see if it *is* possible to analyze doodles.

Reach into your wallet and remove the six business cards. Give one card to each of six spectators taking care to remember who gets which card.

Ask each participating spectator to scribble a doodle on the blank side of his card. It can be anything he likes, ideally the first thing that comes into his mind. When the cards are returned, place them doodle side down and give them a good mix. This enables you to see the pencil-dot markings, which, in turn, will tell you which card belongs to which spectator.

Pick up one of the cards (noting to whom it belongs) and turn it doodle side up. Look at the doodle and, using the knowledge you already possess about its creator, start to give a rapid character reading. You will need to think quickly, but don't worry—the doodles can be very inspirational! At the end of your character assessment show the doodle and say, "I think this sketch was yours, Bill; am I right?" Proceed in a similar manner with the rest of the cards. To prevent an anticlimax, analyze the last two cards together.

It's a splendid trick—don't miss it.

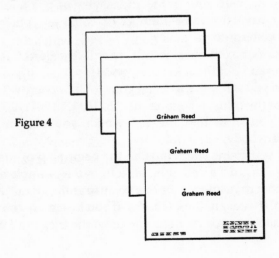

Figure 4

☛ Penny Prediction

Many tricks sound too simple to be effective—and this is one of them. It is, however, quite baffling, and I urge you to try it. You need about fifty one-cent pieces—a colleague of mine carries his in a money bag provided by a friendly bank cashier!

Ask a spectator to reach into the bag and remove a few pennies, "about a dozen or so." He mustn't let you see how many he takes. You then reach into the bag and remove some coins as well. It doesn't matter how many you take, but you *must* have more than the spectator, so take quite a few.

You each count your coins without letting anybody know how many you have. We will assume you have twenty-four coins.

You now make three statements to the spectator:
"I think I have the same number of coins as you plus four extra ones, which we shall disregard, and enough more to bring your total to twenty."

Ask the spectator how many coins he took—let's say fourteen.

Holding your coins in your left hand, start to remove them, one at a time, with your right hand, saying as you do so:
"I said I have the same number of coins as you." Count fourteen coins onto the table.
". . . and four extra ones, which we will disregard." Remove four coins and put them in your pocket.
". . . and enough more to bring your total to twenty." Count the rest of the coins in your hand: "15, 16, 17, 18, 19, 20!"

When you know how the trick works, you wonder how it can fool anybody, but it does.

When you count your coins, at the beginning of the trick, mentally discard a small number (four in the example above). The number remaining is the one you use as the "total" in your statement (twenty in the example). If you take more coins than the spectator, and count them correctly, the trick can't fail.

☛ Coin Divination

Another trick with money. You need five quarters and a French franc, plus six small envelopes, and the most important requirement of them all—a small magnet.

The magnet should be concealed in the curled fingers of your right hand (see figure 5).

Tell your audience that the American and French coins are close in size and weight but you believe you have the ability to locate "foreigners." With this rather vague explanation, you proceed with the trick.

Ask somebody to place one coin in each envelope, seal them, and give them a mix—a *thorough* mix.

Point out how impossible it would be to know, with any certainty, which envelope contains the franc. Pick the envelopes up, one by one, and hold them against your forehead with your right hand. The envelopes help to conceal the magnet. The franc, incidentally, is attracted to the magnet; the quarters are not. Reveal the franc envelope as dramatically as you can and have it opened to verify your statement—another triumph! Quietly slip the magnet into your pocket.

If you wish, you could use the gimmick from Tees for Two to divine the franc envelope.

Figure 5

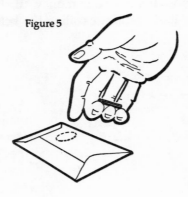

👉 Pricking the Garter

One of the oldest tricks in the book and one of the best. It's a gambling stunt that could start you on the road to a new career! All you need is a leather belt.

To perform the trick, fold the belt in half and start to coil it around itself (see figure 6). The outer part of the belt should be about four inches shorter than the inside half. Point out to a spectator that two loops have formed in the center of the coiled belt. One loop is the genuine center of the belt, and if somebody sticks his finger in this loop and the ends of the belt are pulled, the finger will be caught (you can demonstrate this if you wish). The other loop, however, is *not* the center of the belt, and if this loop is chosen the belt will merely slide around the finger (demonstrate again). Tell the spectator that he has a fifty-fifty chance of finding the genuine center of the belt— and a small wager would seem sporting. All he has to do is stick his finger in the loop that will catch his finger. "Keep your eyes open and you can't lose."

He *can* lose—and he can lose every time if you are sufficiently cruel. When you start to coil the belt make sure you know which is the genuine center of the belt. If the spectator chooses the other loop, you have no problems; merely pull the ends of the belt and ask for your money. If, however, he chooses the center loop, continue coiling the belt and let the

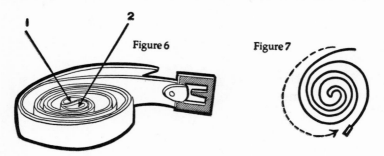

Figure 6

Figure 7

outside end make one more circuit than the inner end (see figure 7). The outer end will now be on the inside—thus altering the center of the belt. The spectator will lose his bet.

Cover the extra circuit of the outer end with your hands— you don't want to be caught cheating people out of their hard-earned money!

☛ Advance Knowledge

I think you will like this cheeky little prediction. You need a 50-cent piece with a round label stuck on its head side. On the label write: I PREDICT YOU WILL CHOOSE THIS COIN. You also need a post card with the message: I PREDICT YOU WILL CHOOSE THE $1 BILL and an envelope with: I PREDICT YOU WILL CHOOSE THE $5 BILL written on the address side. Put the postcard in the envelope and the envelope in your inside pocket. Put the 50-cent piece in a side pocket.

To perform the trick, ask for the loan of a dollar and a $5 bill. Place the bills on a table and put the 50-cent piece next to them tail side up. Remove the envelope from your pocket, making sure you keep the address side to the bottom, out of sight. Place it on the table. Tell the audience you are going to try a simple psychological experiment. Ask a spectator to look at the two bills and the coin, and mentally to select any one. When he has finally decided which he prefers, he is to cover the chosen item with the envelope—you believe you will be able to prove you have anticipated his actions.

The working of the trick should now be obvious:

If the 50-cent piece is chosen, turn it over and reveal the prediction.

If the dollar bill is selected, remove the card from the envelope, and show the message.

If the $5 bill is covered with the envelope, turn the envelope over and show you have correctly predicted the spectator's choice. *You can't fail!*

☛ Pocket-Calculator Puzzlers

If you have a pocket calculator, I think you will find the following stunts to be amusing additions to your repertoire.

(1) Scribble on a piece of paper the number 9 and put the paper, in view, on a table. Don't let anybody see what you have written. Ask somebody to enter any number he likes into the calculator—any number of digits. We will assume:

589721

Then ask him to subtract the same digits in *any* order he wishes:

589721 −
217985

371736 = 27 = 9.

If he adds the digits of the result—*and keeps on adding until he arrives at a single number*—the answer is always nine. Show the piece of paper to show you have correctly predicted his answer.

(2) Write down the number:

12345679

and ask somebody to point to his favorite number. We will assume it's five. Give him the calculator and ask him to multiply 12345679 by 45. The answer is 55555555!

The secret is simple. When a person selects a figure, mentally multiply it by nine. (9 × 5 = 45) and then ask him to multiply 12345679 by the result.

(3) Some of the digits on a pocket calculator look like letters if the calculator is held upside down.

For example 71077345 is a multinational company; 7734 is a hot place; 07734 is a greeting; 7735 is a salesman's priority; 53045 are good for your feet. A little bit of thought will provide many other examples.

FINAL THOUGHTS

Mixing pleasure with business may, on occasion, make sense, but I want to repeat a warning mentioned earlier in the book. We are paid for our on-job activities and not for our private pursuits. It is often possible and desirable to mix the two, but the balance must be right—keep a low magical profile. For example, I have worked in a company for the past eleven years, but very few people know my hobby is conjuring, and only about five colleagues have ever seen me perform any tricks. Magic, in many ways, is like golf: it can be a useful business asset, but never lose sight of your priorities.

DECEIVERS' DICTIONARY

If you listen to several magicians talking to each other, you may feel you are eavesdropping on a crowd of foreigners! Magicians the world over share a unique language consisting of many words and phrases used to describe the various props and moves that enable miracles to be performed. A practical knowledge of magical jargon is essential and I hope you will find the information contained in this chapter of value.

Angle-proof   An angle-proof trick can be performed with the audience surrounding the magician without the danger of the secret being exposed.

Assistant   A person helping the magician.

Billet   A small piece of folded paper usually containing a written message. Often used in mind-reading tricks.

Billet Knife   A hollow knife enabling the performer to insert a billet secretly into an envelope.

Black Art   Refers to the cunning use of black material to disguise a deception.

Book Test   A general term referring to any trick wherein the magician divines a word or words at which a spectator has glanced in a book.

Bottom Deal To deal secretly the bottom card from a pack, while making it appear to be the top card. A favorite ruse of card cheats.

Break A small gap between two playing cards, enabling the performer to locate a selected card.

Bridge A playing card with a slight bend that helps to create a "break" (see Break).

By-Play Amusing patter or actions which, although not magical, help to make a trick more entertaining. Particularly important when performing for children.

Card Box A special box that can vanish or switch a playing card.

Center Tear An extremely clever subtlety used by mentalists and mind readers to gain secret information written on a piece of paper.

Changing Bag A cloth bag with a center partition enabling the performer to exchange secretly one object for another.

Chapeaugraphy An extremely old entertainment in which the performer creates many different hats from a round piece of felt.

Close-Up Mat A small "mat" (usually about 24" by 18") used by close-up performers as a working surface for their tricks. A felt typewriter mat, from any commercial stationer, is ideal.

Cold Deck An unshuffled pack of cards—usually "stacked." Card cheats often secretly exchange their own "cold deck" for the shuffled cards on the table. It's difficult, dangerous, and not recommended!

Complete Cut The deck is cut and the new bottom half placed on top of the original top. You now have a complete deck again, although the order of the cards has been changed.

Confederate A spectator who secretly helps the magician.

Control Card A card whose location in the deck is secretly controlled by the person performing the trick, so that its identity will be revealed to him later on.

Crimp A playing card with a sharp bend in one corner, enabling it to be located by the magician.

Cut The deck is divided into two packets.

Daub A colored substance that is secretly used to mark the back of playing cards. Card cheats use daub to locate high value cards.

Deck or pack A deck or pack of cards.

Devil's Handkerchief A large handkerchief that enables the magician to vanish any small object.

Double-Lift A useful sleight in which two playing cards are displayed, although the audience is aware of only one card.

Dropper A piece of apparatus that secretly drops coins, balls (or whatever) into your hand.

Dye Tube A metal tube that switches one handkerchief for another.

Effect A trick as the audience sees it.

Eight Kings A famous method of stacking a full pack of cards. Miracles can be performed using an Eight-Kings stack.

Escapologist A person who specializes in escaping from chains, handcuffs, et cetera. The most famous one of all is, of course, the great Houdini.

E.S.P. (Extrasensory Perception) A useful phrase often used by mentalists and mind readers.

Expose To reveal the secret of a trick; either deliberately or accidentally—the worst crime any magician can commit.

Faked (Or "gimmicked") Describes an apparently ordinary item (such as a playing card) that has been secretly altered.

False Shuffle A shuffle that looks fair but does *not* mix the cards. There are several different versions, and they are all difficult to perform.

False Cut Although the cards appear to be fairly cut, their order is not altered.

Fan To spread a pack of cards in the shape of a fan.

Fanning Powder A special powder that gives playing cards a smoother surface and makes it easier to fan them evenly.

Feather Flowers Imitation flowers made from feathers. They compress into a small space and are usually used as a production item.

Flap Slates Slates that have a loose flap enabling messages to appear mysteriously. Rarely seen these days.

Flash Accidentally allowing an audience to glimpse something they shouldn't see.

Flash Paper Chemically treated paper which flashes, in a most alarming way, when ignited.

Flourish Movement (with a pack of cards et cetera) which is attractive to the eye.

Force To give an apparently free choice of (say) a playing card, whereas, in reality, the spectator is forced to take a particular card whose identity is known by the performer, sometimes called "magician's choice."

Forcing Pack A faked pack of cards enabling the performer to force a card easily.

French Drop A sleight-of-hand move to vanish a coin or any small object.

Gimmick A secret device or aid.

Gimmicked See Faked.

Glide A sleight-of-hand move with a pack of cards in which the bottom card is apparently placed on the table. In reality, however, it is the second-from-the-bottom card that is dealt.

Houlette A small stand designed to hold a pack of cards in the upright position.

Illusion A trick with large apparatus, usually involving animals or people.

Illusionette A small illusion.

Jog To make a playing card protrude slightly from the pack, enabling it to be easily located.

Jumbo Cards Large playing cards.

Key Card A playing card that is marked, or faked, enabling it to be easily located. Sometimes called a locator card.

Lap To vanish an object, while seated at a table, by secretly dropping it onto your lap.

Loaded Dice Dice that have been weighted on one side to ensure a particular number is thrown more often than it should be.

Locator Card See Key Card.

Magician's Choice See Force.

Manipulator A performer specializing in clever magic, usually with billiard balls, coins, cigarettes, et cetera. The emphasis is on pure skill rather than props and apparatus.

Marked Cards Cards that are marked, on their backs, enabling a person familiar with the system to know the value of a face-down card.

Mechanic's Grip A special way to hold a pack of cards that makes "second deals" much easier. A mechanic is a card cheat who is particularly adept at crooked shuffles and deals.

Mexican Turnover A sleight-of-hand move in which one playing card is exchanged secretly for another.

Misdirection To persuade an audience to look elsewhere when you are performing a secret move.

Move Any sleight or physical deception in which the hands are involved. A double lift, for example, is a move.

One Ahead A clever system used by mind readers which enables the performer apparently to read messages sealed in envelopes.

Opener The first trick in a routine. A good opener should be quick, startling, and eye-catching.

Paddle Move A sleight in which the two sides of (say) a pocket knife are apparently shown, whereas, in reality, one side is shown twice. A very useful move that is not difficult to perform.

Palm To conceal a small item in the palm of your hand.

Patter The words used in your act. A patter act is a magician who talks during his performance, whereas, in contrast, a manipulator is often silent, apart from background music.

Preparation The work necessary to prepare a trick before you can perform it for an audience.

Production Item Anything that compresses into a small space and is suitable for producing from "empty" boxes.

Props A general term covering all your theatrical properties—tricks, tables, etc.

Pull A device that vanishes small objects by pulling them up your sleeve.

Rope Special soft rope used by magicians. Obtainable from most magic dealers.

Routine A carefully blended selection of tricks. A good routine starts with an eye-catching opener; the tricks are varied (although possibly with one theme—such as cards); and the routine ends with a strong, memorable climax

Second Deal Although the performer apparently deals the top card of the pack, in reality it is the second card that is played. Often used by crooked gamblers.

Self-working A trick that is not difficult to perform.

Selling a Trick Gaining the maximum entertainment value from a trick—performing it superbly well.

Shiner A small mirror (about ½ inch in diameter) which is concealed in the hand. It enables a card cheat to see the value of face-down cards as he deals from the pack.

Short Card A card that is fractionally shorter than the rest of the pack. Its reduced length enables it to be easily located. See Key Card.

Silent Act An act without patter—usually with a musical background.

Silk A silk (or similar) scarf.

Sleeve To vanish a small object up the sleeve.

Sleight A skillful move.

Slicked Card A playing card that has been polished on its face (with Simoniz), enabling a card cheat to cut the deck at the slicked card. "He was using a set of slicked aces."

Spring Flowers Imitation flowers that compress into a very small space. Usually produced from "empty" boxes.

Stacked Pack A pack of cards in a prearranged order. See Cold Deck.

Steal To remove something secretly. For example, the performer may appear to put a coin under a cup, wheras, in reality, he steals it without the audience's realizing the deception that has taken place.

Stooge See Confederate.

Strippers A pack of cards that has one end slightly narrower than the other. If a card is reversed, it can easily be located and "stripped" out of the pack.

Sucker Trick A trick in which the audience is led to believe they have spotted the secret—and then the performer reveals he has deliberately deceived them.

Switch To exchange one object for another.

Talking Any noise that accidentally exposes the working of a trick—for example, two coins clinking together when the audience believes the performer has only one coin.

Thick Card A card that is thicker than the rest of the pack, making it easy to locate. See Key Card.

Thumb Palm To conceal any small item by secretly gripping it under the base of the thumb.

Thumb Tip An imitation thumb tip that fits on the end of the performer's thumb (rather like a thimble), enabling him to vanish small objects.

Troublewit A large piece of strong, specially folded paper with which the performer is able to make many amusing shapes.

Vent Abbreviation for Ventriloquist.

Wand A black stick with white tips, often used by magicians as an aid to misdirection.

Wax A specially made sticky substance that enables the magician to stick two playing cards together.

Well A hole in the top of the performer's table, into which small objects can be secretly dropped.

9

TESTED
TRICKERY

Most readers will wish to expand their repertoire, and the aim of this chapter is to provide brief details of just a few of the many tricks sold by the magical dealers. The comments should help to ensure that the reader avoids tricks that are unsuitable and spends his or her money on effective tricks within his capabilities.

Thanks are due to my good friend, Martin Marshall, for his help in compiling the list of tricks.

Aerial Fishing A superb trick in which the performer apparently produces live goldfish on the end of a fishing line that is cast into the audience! Difficult to obtain and not easy to perform. Leave it to the professionals.

Antigravity Glasses Three glasses are placed, mouth down, on a thin sheet of Plexiglas. Everything is then turned upside down, but the glasses stay in position without apparent support. A good visual trick for small or large audiences—adults or children.

Any Drink Called For The performer shows a large kettle and several glasses. Members of the audience call out various drinks, and the magician pours all the requested drinks from the same kettle! A very nice trick but not recommended for beginners.

Appearing Cane A cane suddenly appears out of midair! Easy to do and very, very effective. Suitable for medium/large audiences—children or adults. Highly recommended.

Balloon Penetration A large needle is pushed, visibly, through a balloon—and it doesn't burst! Looks impossible to perform. An ideal opener for children or adults. Strongly recommended.

Bending Glass A sheet of glass, in a wooden frame, is placed in a paper bag which is then bent backward and forward. Knives are also plunged through the center (?) of the glass. At the end of the trick the sheet of glass is shown to be undamaged. The trick is dramatic and not difficult to do. Suitable for medium/large audiences of adults.

Bill Tube A borrowed $5 bill vanishes and immediately reappears in a locked metal tube, which can be examined by members of the audience. A baffling trick that is ideal for adult audiences. Highly recommended.

Blendo Several silk scarves are thrown into the air and they change into one large multicolored scarf. A colorful opener suitable for medium/large audiences of children or adults. Recommended.

Boomerangs Two wooden boomerangs are shown to be the same length and then they start to get bigger—and then they shrink! The trick is a lot of fun and highly recommended for any audience of children.

Botania A colorful production of a large bouquet of flowers. Very dramatic but difficult to obtain. Rather expensive.

Brain-Wave Pack A pack of cards, in its case, is shown and a spectator shouts out the name of any card he likes. The pack is removed from the case—and the cards are facing the same way, except for one, and it's the chosen card! A superb opening trick for any adult audience. Enthusiastically recommended.

Brass Nut Release A large brass nut is threaded onto a piece of string. Two spectators hold the ends of the string and, under cover of a handkerchief, the performer magically removes the nut. Everything can be examined. An excellent close-up trick for children or adults. Highly recommended.

Broomstick Levitation A girl is suspended, horizontally, on two broomsticks. One of the broomsticks is removed but, inexplicably, she remains floating in midair! A very effective illusion performed by many professional magicians.

Card in Balloon An inflated balloon is placed on a thin stand. A card is chosen and returned to the pack. Bang! The balloon bursts and, in its place, is the chosen card. A superb trick for any audience of children. Enthusiastically recommended.

Card Castle The performer scatters a pack of cards onto his table and covers them with a large cloth. The center of the cloth is pulled upward to reveal a large card castle. Can be expensive but worth the cost—a spectacular finale for your act. Suitable for medium/large audiences of children or adults. Highly recommended.

Cards from Pocket A pack of cards is shuffled and half the pack placed in your left pocket—the other half in your right pocket. Spectators call out the names of playing cards and you rapidly reach into your pockets, removing the chosen cards! *Not* easy to do, but well worth the effort. The trick could make your reputation. Ideal for medium/large audiences of adults.

Card Sword A card is chosen and returned to the pack. The performer shows a long, slim sword, the cards are thrown into the air, the performer stabs at the cards, and the chosen card is seen to be impaled on the tip of the sword! Card swords are rather scarce these days. If you get the chance to buy one, do so. The trick is highly recommended for medium/large audiences of children or adults.

Card in Wallet A chosen card vanishes from the pack and is discovered inside a sealed envelope, which, in turn, is inside a zippered wallet. A splendid trick that is highly recommended for any adult audience.

Chain Handcuffs The magician's wrists are securely fastened in a pair of impressive chain handcuffs. He turns his back to the audience for a second, and, wonder of wonders, he's free! A very powerful trick with which to finish your act. Highly recommended for medium/large audiences of adults.

Chair-Back Suspension A lady from the audience lies on a wooden plank that is supported on the backs of two chairs. One of the chairs is removed, but she remains suspended in midair! A splendid illusionette that is ideal for a stage performance. Not cheap but it could make your reputation. Strongly recommended for medium/large adult audiences.

Chinese Compass   Arrows, on each side of a small plastic plaque, keep mysteriously pointing in different directions. Recommended for small audiences of children or adults.

Chinese Sticks   Two rods, each with a cord running through one end, are shown. If one cord is pulled, the other one reacts even though the rods are well apart. A difficult trick to make entertaining; spend your cash on something else.

Chop Cup   A superb effect in which the magician performs the most incredible tricks with a metal cup and a small ball. Not easy to do, and it can be an expensive trick to buy. Nevertheless, it is unreservedly recommended for small/medium audiences of children or adults.

Clippo   A long strip of paper is cut in half and immediately restored. Easy to do; a good trick for any audience of children or adults.

Coin in Bottle   A borrowed 10-cent piece magically appears inside a bottle, but the neck is too narrow for the coin to be removed! A very good trick but difficult to perform . Not recommended for beginners.

Color-Changing Knife   A small pocket knife keeps changing its color. Another excellent trick that isn't easy to perform. Not recommended for beginners.

Color-Changing Shoelace   The magician strokes a white shoelace which immediately changes color. The trick is recommended as an ideal opener for small/medium audiences of children or adults.

Color-Changing Silk   Similar to Color-Changing Shoelace, but using a small silk handkerchief. Another good opener.

Copper/Silver Transposition   A penny and a dime keep changing places in an inexplicable manner. The trick is first-class but not easy to perform. Unsuitable for beginners.

Cups and Balls   One of the classics of magic: small balls vanish, reappear, and multiply under three metal cups. Extremely difficult to perform. Save your money!

Cut-and-Restored Rope   Another magical classic of which there are several different versions. A good cut-and-restored-rope routine is ideal entertainment for any audience of children or adults. Enthusiastically recommended.

Devano Rising Card Chosen cards rise from the pack—and the performer is nowhere near! A beautiful trick invented by a well-known member of the Magic Circle. Suitable for any adult audience. Highly recommended.

Die Box A classic "sucker" trick in which the magician vanishes a large wooden die in a double-fronted box. The audience think they know how it's done—but the magician has the last laugh! Rather expensive but well worth the price if you can afford it. Enthusiastically recommended for medium/large audiences of children.

Diminishing Cards A fan of cards that get smaller, and smaller and smaller until, finally, they vanish. Not recommended for beginners.

Dippy the Duck A large wooden model of a bird finds spectator's cards after they have been shuffled back into the pack. A magnificent trick. Highly recommended for medium/large audiences of children or adults.

Dollhouse Illusion A classic illusion in which a dollhouse is shown to be empty—the door is closed—and suddenly, the roof bursts open to reveal the magician's assistant! Particularly suitable for a stage performance.

Dove Pan A large metal pan is shown to be empty. The lid is put on, a wave of the wand, and the pan is now overflowing with silk scarves, flowers, et cetera. A highly recommended trick with which to finish a routine for children.

Dye Box Colored Silk scarves are placed into a soap powder box—and they turn white. An amusing trick that is recommended for medium/large audiences of children.

Egg Bag An egg constantly vanishes and reappears in a small cloth bag. A difficult trick to perform convincingly.

Evaporated Milk A large quantity of milk is poured into a paper cone. The cone is crushed and thrown into the audience—the milk has vanished! A first-class trick for medium/large audiences of children or adults. Strongly recommended.

Floating Ball   A large metal ball floats in midair all over the stage. A visual and beautiful trick that can only be performed on stage; it is also difficult to perform. Not recommended for beginners.

Head Chopper   A spectator puts his head in a realistic guillotine—the blade descends—but the spectator is unharmed. An excellent illusionette; highly recommended for medium/large adult audiences.

Himber Ring   Three signet rings are borrowed from members of the audience—and apparently linked together! An incredible trick but rather expensive for the average beginner.

Himber Wallet   A very useful prop that enables you to perform many first-class tricks. Strongly recommended. Every magician should own one.

Hypnotized Rope   A piece of rope is hypnotized and immediately goes very stiff; a snap of the fingers and it's limp again. Easy to do.

Just Chance   Two spectators are given the choice of any one of three envelopes. When they are opened the envelopes contain only worthless pieces of paper, whereas the envelope left for the magician contains a $10 bill! A good trick that is recommended for any medium/large audience of adults.

Leg Chopper   Similar to Head Chopper.

Linking Rings   A classic of magic in which large steel rings link and unlink in the most amazing way. The trick is difficult to perform but well worth the effort. Enthusiastically recommended for medium/large audiences of adults or children.

Magic Welding   Small steel rings become magically linked together into a long chain. An effective trick for medium/large audiences of adults or children.

Mail-Bag Escape   The performer is securely locked inside a large sack—but he escapes in seconds. A dramatic trick that could make your reputation. Recommended for large adult audiences.

Mirror Box   A good prop that enables you to produce numerous silk scarves from an empty box. Particularly suitable for medium/large audiences of children.

Multiplying Billiard Ball The performer shows a billiard ball which, eventually, multiplies to eight balls. Difficult to do and not worth the effort.

Mutiplying Bottles Numerous bottles are produced from two large tubes. The trick is expensive and not recommended for beginners.

Nudist Pack A pack of blank playing cards is shown—magically the performer "prints" faces and backs—the pack is now normal. A good opener for medium/large audiences of adults or children.

Okito Coin Box A small metal box that enables you to perform several tricks with coins. Not for beginners.

Rough and Smooth Pack A very useful pack of cards which enables you to force a card very easily.

Serpent Silk A long silk scarf, tied in a knot, visibly unties itself. A splendid trick that is an excellent opener for large audiences of adults or children.

Siberian Transport Chain The performer's wrists are securely chained together—in seconds he escapes. A very good trick; recommended for medium/large adult audiences.

Six-Card Repeat The magician shows six playing cards. He throws three away—he still has six. He throws three more away—and he still has six cards. And so it goes on. Another good opener for medium/large audiences of adults or children.

Sympathetic Silks Six silk scarves knot and unknot in sympathy. A pleasant trick with plenty of eye appeal. Recommended for medium/large audiences of adults or children.

Thumb Tie Although the performer's thumbs are tightly tied together, large rings magically penetrate onto his arms. A very spectacular trick that could help to make your reputation. Not easy to do but well worth the effort. Strongly recommended for medium/large adult audiences.

Torn-and-Restored Newspaper A newspaper is torn into several pieces—and immediately restored. A good opener for large audiences of adults or children.

Unequal Ropes   Three ropes constantly change their length—magically! Another excellent opener that is recommended for medium/large audiences of adults or children.

Vanishing Cane   A robust cane visibly vanishes! A superb trick that is enthusiastically recommended for medium/large audiences of adults or children.

Wrist Chopper   Similar to Head Chopper.

Zigzag Illusion   A magnificent stage illusion in which a girl is divided into three parts. Created by one of England's most prolific magical inventors, the late Robert Harbin.

Zombie   A large metal ball floats in midair. Not easy to do. Save your money.

USEFUL ADDRESSES

DEALERS

California

Farmers Market and Fun Shop
6333 West Third Avenue
Los Angeles, California 90055

Hollywood Magic Inc.
6614 Hollywood Boulevard
Los Angeles, California 90028

Illinois

Magic Inc.
5082 N. Lincoln
Chicago, Illinois 60625

Massachusetts

Paul M. Tosi Magician's Supplies
533 N. Main Street
Boston, Massachusetts 02139

Michigan

Abbott's Magic Mfg. Co.
Colon, Michigan 49040

The Secret Magic and Joke Shop
229 Merle Hay Mall
Detroit, Michigan 48226

New Jersey

Ken's Magic Shop
28-01 Broadway
Fair Lawn, New Jersey 07410

Kenzini's Magic Palace
  Showroom
954-B Stuyvesant Avenue
Union, New Jersey 07083

New Mexico

Marvelo's Magic Shop
483 Brown Street
Albuquerque, New Mexico 87101

New York

Circle Magic Inc.
1661 Broadway
New York, New York 10019

Hornmann Magic Co.
304 W. 34th Street
New York, New York 10001

Magic Towne House Inc.
1026 Third Avenue
New York, New York 10021

Louis Tannen Inc.
1540 Broadway
New York, New York 10036

Westchester Magician Supplies
20 Columbus Avenue
Tuckahoe, New York 10707

Tennessee

Magic Mart
7900 Luxmore Drive
Knoxville, Tennessee 37919

Smart Fred—Magician
1210 Eighth Avenue S.
Nashville, Tennessee 37202

MAGAZINES

Genii
Box 36068
Los Angeles, California 90036

Hocus-Pocus
1026 Third Avenue
New York, New York 10021

Linking Ring
International Brotherhood of
  Magicians
Kenton, Ohio 43326

Magic Cauldron
700 Glenview Avenue S. W.
Glen Burnie, Maryland 21061

M-U-M (Magic, Unity, Might)
Society of American Magicians
c/o Herbert B. Donns
National Secretary
66 Marked Tree Road
Needham, Massachusetts 02192

The New Tops
Abbott's Magic Mfg. Co.
Colon, Michigan 49040

MAGIC CLUBS AND SHOWPLACES

International Brotherhood of
Magicians
Kenton, Ohio 43326

The Magic Castle
7001 Franklin Avenue
Hollywood, California 90028

The Magic Circle
84 Chenies Mews
London WC1, England

Magic Towne House
1026 Third Avenue
New York, New York 10021

Mostly Magic
53 Carmine Street
New York, New York 10014

Society of American Magicians
Att: Frank Buslovich
Lock Drawer 789
Lynn, Massachusetts 01903

RECOMMENDED READING

Whether you perform once a year or once a day, a few carefully selected books will help to increase your enjoyment and your ability. The newcomer to magic is often amazed at the tremendous amount of conjuring books that are available in local shops or from specialist dealers. The wide variety of titles can be confusing, and even glancing at the book, before buying it, doesn't guarantee it will be a worthwhile purchase. Many useless books look extremely attractive. On the other hand, quite a few superb books are badly produced and rather expensive.

In the following list I have concentrated on books that contain good practical tricks and at the same time represent value for money. Apart from being fun to read and a source of useful ideas, most conjuring books are an excellent investment: they become scarce quite quickly and their second-hand cost is often much higher than their original price.

Anderson, George B. *Magic Digest.*
Chicago: Follett, 1972.

One of the best-known names in British magic once said to me: *Magic Digest* is the best magical book available today. That may seem quite a strong statement, but I must say that the book is one of my personal favorites, and I wish it had been available when I first started performing magic. George B. Anderson combines his twin talents of magical entertainer and professional writer to give you a book that contains some splendid tricks, and they are all beautifully described. The tricks use props that can be found in most homes, and they are all relatively easy to perform. The book is enthusiastically recommended.

Beal, George. *Playing Cards and Their Story.*
New York: Arco, 1974.

George Beal's book will interest anybody who is eager to learn more about the fascinating history of playing cards. It is beautifully illustrated with examples of cards from all over the world.

Christopher, Milbourne. *Houdini – A Pictorial Life.*
New York: Thomas Y. Crowell, 1976.

Anybody interested in conjuring should have a working knowledge about the greatest magician/escapologist of all time—Harry Houdini. Milbourne Christopher's book is a fascinating collection of facts and pictures, and I recommend it without reservation.

Christopher, Milbourne. *The Illustrated History of Magic.*
New York: Thomas Y. Crowell, 1973.

Milbourne Christopher is a charming American magician/writer who has penned some of the most significant magical books of our time. *The Illustrated History of Magic* is a book you *must* buy. There are no tricks in it, but it is without doubt the most comprehensive (and most interesting) history of conjuring ever published. From the priests of ancient Egypt to modern-day miracle workers—it's all here. Numerous prints, photographs, and engravings illustrate the book. *Don't miss it.*

Fulves, Karl. *Self-Working Card Tricks.*
New York: Dover, 1976.

This slim booklet contains some of the most entertaining card tricks ever created. Take my tip and buy a copy.

Garcia, Frank, and George Schindler. *Magic with Cards.*
New York: David McKay, 1975.

Another splendid card book; all the tricks are very easy to do. Garcia is a well-known card expert and Schindler a performer and a teacher. They make a first-class team.

Gibson, Walter B. *The Complete Illustrated Book of Card Magic: The Principles & Techniques Fully Revealed in Text and Photographs.* Garden City, N.Y.: Doubleday, 1969.

Walter B. Gibson is one of the world's most prolific magical writers, and this book is a masterpiece. If you can afford only one book on card tricks, this must be *the* one. Hundreds of tricks are described; hundreds of pages and scores of photographic illustrations. A truly magnificent book that will give you (and your audiences) a lifetime of pleasure.

Hugard, Jean, and Frederick Braue. *Expert Card Technique.* New York: Dover, 1975.

This is a classical book of card tricks, but be warned: many of them are difficult. If, however, you want to progress, the book is well worth buying.

Lorayne, Harry. *The Magic Book: The Complete Beginner's Guide to Anytime, Anywhere, Sleight-of-Hand Magic.* New York: Putnam, 1977.

Harry Lorayne is a professional entertainer who has many books to his credit. He writes in an interesting way, and all his books are like personal instruction—you feel as though he were sitting with you. *The Magic Book* is splendid value. Suffice it to say that I own *two* copies: one I keep on my book shelves and the other travels with me everywhere I go. I can't think of a better testimony than that.
The book concentrates on tricks with everyday objects—playing cards, coins, et cetera. Highly recommended.

Majax, Gerard. *Secrets of the Card Sharps.* New York: Sterling, 1977.

This book is written by one of the foremost card experts, who has made a lifelong study of card cheats all over the world and has many fascinating stories to tell. Dozens of photographs graphically illustrate the various techniques used by card cheats—techniques that magicians can, and do, use. A very interesting book that could save you a lot of money or start you on the road to a new career.

Rydell, Wendy, and George Gilbert. *The Great Book of Magic.*
New York: Harry N. Abrams, 1976.

This is an expensive book but well worth the cost. The first part
consists of a comprehensive history of magic with many interesting
anecdotes and numerous illustrations, many in full color. The second
half of the book contains a first-class selection of tricks, all fully
described with some of the best line drawings I have ever seen in a
magic book. Most of the tricks are for stage performance, and this is
valuable because many conjuring books concentrate on close-up
tricks. An excellent book for the beginner, especially for the magician
who wants to perform for children and/or on stage.

Schindler, George. *Magic with Everyday Objects.*
Briarcliff Manor, N. Y. : Stein and Day, 1980.

One of my favorite books—highly recommended. George Schindler
is an experienced entertainer, and his book contains dozens of excellent tricks. They are all practical and, even more important, they are
all entertaining.

INDEX
OF TRICKS